We hope you enjoy this book.
Please return or renew it by the due date.
You can renew it at **www.norfolk.gov.uk/libraries**
or by using our free library app. Otherwise you can
phone **0344 800 8020** - please have your library
card and pin ready.
You can sign up for email reminders too.

NORFOLK COUNTY COUNCIL
LIBRARY AND INFORMATION SERVICE

NORFOLK ITEM

3 0129 08444 7540

Published in Great Britain by Hashtag Press 2020

Text © Yousra Imran 2020
Cover Design © Anne Glenn 2020
Cover Photograph © Agata Tatiana Urbanska 2020

The moral right of the author has been asserted

A CIP catalogue for this book is available from the British Library.

ISBN 978-1-9162864-9-8

Typeset in Garamond Classic 11.25/14 by Blaze Typesetting

Printed in Great Britain by Clays Ltd, Elcograf S.p.A.

Hashtag PRESS

HASHTAG PRESS BOOKS
Hashtag Press Ltd
Kent, England, United Kingdom
Email: info@hashtagpress.co.uk
Website: www.hashtagpress.co.uk
Twitter: @hashtag_press

*This book is dedicated to every girl and woman who was told
that their story was not important enough to tell.
Your voice is important.
Your story is important.
Keep on telling it until they listen.*

ACKNOWLEDGEMENTS

There have been a number of people throughout my life who have stood by me through thick and thin and helped me find the strength that ultimately led me to becoming the woman I am today—a woman who strives to be fearless in the face of the patriarchy.

I would like to thank Reem Ayed, a special friend who was there for me throughout my university years and beyond, who followed the principle of telling it like it is, and who let me cry in her car and living room many a time.

Thank you to my best friends and favourite couple Selina Farooqui and Rami Khleif, who have been my number-one supporters and patient bearers of all my antics.

Thank you to a number of teachers and lecturers from my secondary school and university, who were there for me during troubling times at home and who instilled confidence in me to keep on writing and never give up on my dream of independence. They are Rachael Green, Andrew Martin, Dr Amira Sonbol, Dr Muneera Al-Ghadeer, Dr Mazhar Al-Zoby and Dr Mohanalakshmi Rajakumar.

Thank you to Mona El-Tahawy, the most fearless feminist and warrior against the patriarchy I know, who encouraged me in person to write this book and whose own books inspired me to tell my story and to truly believe that my voice matters.

A massive thank you to Helen Lewis and Abiola Bello, who chose my book to win Hashtag Press 2020 and turned my dream of becoming a published author into a reality. Thank you Helen and Abiola for all the hard work you've put into bringing this book to life and for your continuous support.

And finally, thank you to my mother and father. We may not always see eye to eye, but you continue to love me and support me no matter what.

NOTE TO THE READER

It is important to remember not to discount the experience of a woman if it is not an experience of your own.

I have drawn on my own life experiences and the experiences of other Arabs who were born and brought up in the West and moved to the Middle East as teenagers when writing this novel.

This is the story of one British Arab woman's journey to finding herself while living in a patriarchal society where men—and sometimes women—mix their culture with religion in order to wrongfully control girls and women.

A glossary of Arabic words and phrases is available in alphabetical order at the end of this book.

This book contains some sensitive topics which readers under the age of sixteen may find distressing, including discussions of rape, coercive behaviour, self-harm, domestic abuse and sexual abuse.

"Are you sure you want to go on national television wearing red lipstick? You know what your dad will say."

"Mum, are you being serious? Do you think at twenty-nine I'm going to let Baba tell me off for wearing red lipstick?" I shook my head in disbelief. "I'm going to have to hang up Mum, the next stop is mine."

I pressed the red *Stop* button in front of me.

"Good luck sweetie. FaceTime me in the evening and let me know how your interview went. I'm so proud of you Sara," Mum replied.

We waved goodbye at each other before ending our daily video call.

Sophie, the BBC journalist who was interviewing me, had asked whether I wanted to meet at the BBC Studios or a nearby café. I had been inside the BBC Studios for an interview before and found it too intimidating so I went for the second option. We agreed to meet at a Caffè Nero a couple of streets away.

My phone vibrated.

Hiya Sara! Running a couple of minutes late. My last meeting finished later than it was supposed to. So sorry. See you very soon! Sophie

No need for me to hurry then.

I strolled leisurely along the main street, busy at this time of the day when everyone was escaping their offices for lunch at the nearest Pret, Costa or Starbucks.

Once I got to Caffè Nero, I immediately noticed that there

were a couple of comfy chairs and a low, round table tucked away at the far end of the room. I marched over, determined to grab them before anyone else did.

I recognised Sophie as she sauntered past the queue of people at the counter, a few minutes later. We had been following each other on Twitter for ages before she sent me a DM asking me to be the star of her new project.

She was wearing a little black leather jacket, over a calf-length polka dot dress, which was definitely from Zara, designer sunglasses perched on top of her thick golden-brown hair. She looked exactly like the type of woman I aspired to be when I was in my mid-twenties.

I have golden-brown hair too, although it's not my natural colour. But no one would know that because I keep my hair tied up in a messy bun under my *hijab*.

"Sara! So good to finally meet you. Can I get you anything? A coffee? Cake?" Sophie asked, rummaging through her handbag. She pulled out her wallet along with a small digital voice recorder.

"Nice to meet you too and I'm fine, thanks. I ate just before I left home," I replied.

"I'll get us both some water then—don't want us getting thirsty from all the talking we're about to do!" Sophie exclaimed. She was as vibrant and enthusiastic in person as she was on social media.

I scrolled through social media and a few minutes later, a bottle of water was thrust under my nose.

"The documentary is going to be a two-part special," Sophie explained, as she sat down.

"A special...on my life?" I asked. It was still hard to believe.

"I would do a whole series on your life if I had the budget!" Sophie said, grinning from ear to ear. "It's not every day that you meet a British woman who has lived under the guardianship system and is open to telling the world what life is like for women in Saudi Arabia, Qatar and the UAE. But the head of my department told me the budget for this affords us two episodes, so we're going to need to squeeze it all into a couple of hours."

"Is that even possible?" I asked her. "There's just so much that's happened. So much I have to tell you."

"We'll make it possible, don't worry. After all, film-making is my job," she said with a wink. "Now, this isn't a formal question-answer interview. I want you to tell me your story. You choose what you want to share. I will only ask questions if I need clarification. My videographer, John, will be joining us later to get some basic shots of you walking down the street."

"Where do I start?"

"How about you start from where it all began? Here, in your home city, London."

Baba

The Egyptian community in the capital was a close-knit bunch of families who mainly lived in North West London. Just as in most ethnic minority communities, everybody knew each other.

The glue that held our community together was our fathers who had emigrated as fresh university graduates from Egypt in the 1980s. They would bring their young Egyptian wives along with them, or arrive as bachelors who quickly snapped up a wave of young English women who had converted to Islam. The children produced from these marriages grew up together and called each other's mums *khalto*, which in Arabic means auntie. Our dads were called *amu*, meaning uncle.

My father, who I call Baba, moved to London in the late 1980s. He was another engineering graduate, in a saturated sea of engineers in Cairo, who thought he would have better career prospects in England. He was one of the Egyptians who bagged himself a young English convert. My mother.

Baba had a close relationship to the *amu*s. In Islam, we are taught that other Muslims are our brothers and sisters. It was safe to say that Baba took that very seriously, so much so that growing up—Mum, my siblings (Ahmed, Saffa, and Abdullah) and I often felt that he put the *amu*s before us.

When he was not at work as a salesman at an electronics store run by another Egyptian, he was at one of the *amu*s' houses. At home, he would regularly host the *amu*s at our place.

One of Mum's biggest pet peeves with Baba was that he took the *amu*s' advice over hers. It was as if he did not trust the advice of a woman. It constantly landed us in trouble.

For example, when his Egyptian boss—who lived in a lovely mansion in North West London—advised Baba to give up our privately rented flat and tell Westminster Council that we were homeless, instead of getting a three-bedroom council house like his boss promised would happen, the council gave us a poky two-bedroom flat in Pimlico.

I'm not talking about the posh part of Pimlico with the rows of terraced marble-white houses. It was a dingy council estate in the early 1990s, where our neighbours were drug dealers, paedophiles and prostitutes, and definitely not the upper-class well-to-do MPs as neighbours Baba had hoped for.

It turned out to be the first of many instances in which Baba's insistence to take the *amu*s' advice put us in a far worse situation.

Baba was an ambitious man. He had always wanted to be a 'somebody.' He achieved this by becoming a pillar of religion within the Egyptian community. From as early as I can remember, he was the host of Qur'an gatherings, known in Arabic as *halaqas*.

In these gatherings—which were strictly male-only as most Muslims don't encourage the free mixing of men and women—Baba would teach the attendees how to read the Qur'an and then they would discuss its meaning, along with the myriad Islamic rules and laws, which are called *fiqh* and *shari'ah*.

Baba wasn't a scholar, but you would have thought he was one by the way everyone in the Egyptian community consulted him for Islamic rulings. The *amu*s called him *ustaadh*, a term of respect, which means teacher.

When the *amu*s came to our little council flat for a *halaqa*, Mum would be banished to her bedroom. She was not allowed to be in plain sight of the men. Being seen would have been *'eyb* or shameful.

It was her job to cook them a huge dinner to eat after their *halaqa*. She would spend hours in the kitchen cooking and the *amu*s would demolish it all within 10 minutes.

Mum never complained. Baba had taught her most of what she knew about Islam and one of the key things was that a Muslim woman should always obey her husband.

This religiosity extended to us kids. We were enrolled into Arabic School on Saturdays the minute each of us turned five years old. Ask any British Arab and they'll tell you how much they loathed Arabic School. For six hours on a Saturday you would sit learning Arabic grammar, Islamic Studies and the Qur'an from strict Libyan teachers who either couldn't understand English or pretended they couldn't.

The teachers were barbaric doling out medieval punishments for the slightest misdemeanour. Being hit on your knuckles with a ruler, or having to stand with one arm and leg raised were among their favourite punishments.

I grew up wondering how they got away with hitting children in Britain.

Saffa, Ahmed and I would cry every Saturday morning,

begging Baba to let us stay at home and have a full two-day weekend like English children, but he showed no mercy. He would have to pull Saffa's legs as she held on to the living room coffee table with both hands, suspending her in the air so that she looked like Superman.

Rebel

Boys. A sticky topic for all Arab fathers.

I was allowed to be friends with the *amus'* sons. They were practically my cousins. Our friendships were platonic. Even as we grew older and approached our teenage years, we knew that some of the more daring Egyptian boys and girls who Baba said had, "gone off the right track" were dating, but they dated people outside the Egyptian community. The friendships of the boys and girls within our close-knit community remained innocent.

Baba had not waited for me to become a teenager to have 'the talk' about dating. He drilled it into me from the age of eight.

"Boyfriends are *haram*," he would repeat.

Haram and *halal*—what is forbidden and what is allowed in Islam. They were the two most well-used words within Baba's vocabulary. If a kissing scene came on the television, we had to change the channel straight away.

If we were at Regent's Park with Baba and saw a couple rolling about on the grass we were automatically told, "Look the other way, they are *haram*. If you look, your eyeballs will testify against you on the Day of Judgement."

I had strict instructions for high school. I was allowed to have male friends as long as they didn't become boyfriends. Any raging pubescent hormones were to be suppressed until I was old enough to get married. According to Baba that would not be until he saw my university degree in my hand. That was the Egyptian way. You get your degree and then you get married. Whether as a woman you actually got a job and use that degree would be the decision of your husband.

To be honest there weren't any boys at school that I fancied anyway. They were mostly Christian and as a Muslim I already knew that even if I had taken a liking to any of them, it would be a waste of time. Muslim women aren't allowed to marry a non-Muslim man unless he converts to Islam first.

*

Baba controlled everything. What we read, listened to and watched. Arabic music was allowed. English music was not. When *Top of the Pops* came on, we had to change channels. His reason was that Arabic songs were innocent, while English songs were filthy, and that the obscenities in English music made it *haram*.

At school, my friends would be singing the latest tunes during break time, and I couldn't join in their sing-a-long because I had no idea what they were singing! I didn't know the latest Spice Girls or Britney Spears tracks.

As I entered my teenage years, I started to question Baba about his music ban.

"*Haram* is *haram*," Baba would say. "The words in the songs are from the devil. They will have a bad effect on your soul. If you do not stop complaining I will forbid Arabic music too."

So, like any normal teenager's reaction to their parents forbidding something, I began to rebel.

My friends would make copies of their cassette tapes and give them to me. I hid the tapes in a blue plastic storage box under school textbooks in my room. I took them out and listened to them on my Walkman with my headphones plugged in.

Since I was allowed to listen to Arabic music I never thought Baba would doubt that I was listening to anything else. But on a Sunday afternoon, as I sat on my bed with my earphones plugged in, Baba marched in to my room, yanked my earphones out of my ears and put an earphone to his ear. I had been listening to *Oops I Did It Again* by Britney Spears

"Are there more tapes?" Baba asked and I lied and shook my head.

I thought I had fooled him but later that evening, while I was having a bath, he raided my personal belongings, including the blue plastic box, and confiscated my cassettes.

As soon as I had the opportunity, I complained to Mum about it.

"Can't you try and convince him?" I pleaded. "Songs are just words; they don't have any effect on me."

"I can try but I can't promise anything," Mum said. "You know I'm rubbish at persuading him to do anything."

Whether she had or hadn't talked to him, the rules didn't change. So I found other ways to listen to music.

Baba had taken away all my tapes, but not my Walkman,

which had the radio. So I started listening to Kiss FM instead, which opened up a whole world of artists and genres. I started off liking the mainstream artists and girl bands of the day: Pink, Mis-Teeq and Destiny's Child. Then I developed a liking for rock music. Red Hot Chili Peppers, The Calling and Linkin Park were my favourite bands.

The battle to listen to English music continued until I finally won at age fourteen.

My best friend at school, Faima, asked me what I wanted for my birthday and I told her that I wanted The Calling's album.

"Is that a good idea?" she asked nervously. "Seeing as your dad doesn't like you listening to English music."

"Well, it will be a test of how heartless my dad can be. If he isn't heartless, he will allow me to keep my birthday present," I said defiantly.

Turns out that Baba was not as heartless as I thought or maybe he had just had enough and caved in. The Calling's first album, *Wherever You Will Go*, was my first official item of music.

Now that I was allowed to listen to English music, my brother Ahmed started to dabble in it too. We would put our pocket money together, walk to HMV on our local high street on a Sunday afternoon and buy CDs. We explored different artists together.

Ahmed, who was only eleven, was developing a strong liking for rap and grime. He was obsessed with Eminem and So Solid Crew.

We still weren't allowed to play music out loud at home, but we were allowed to listen to it with our headphones plugged in, which Ahmed and I agreed was a good compromise.

*

There were happy memories too. Although Baba was strict and not at home a lot of the time, he would spend Sundays with us. The day would start with him cooking up a big Egyptian breakfast: fried eggs with lots of black pepper and salty cured meat called *basturma*, Egyptian falafel called *tamayya*, and *fool*, which is mashed fava beans mixed with tahini.

We would then get washed and changed and he would take us out. Usually it was for a trip to Regent's Park followed by an ice cream and a stroll along Edgware Road.

While we were at Primary School, Baba went back to university part-time to study for his Master's degree and changed career paths to publishing and media. He left his job as a salesman and joined the world of Arabic newspapers, many of which had offices in London.

Egyptian men are proud. Having a degree in petroleum engineering and a job as a salesman hadn't gone down well with him, but back then it was the best job he could find as a new immigrant. Now, as an editor in a highly-regarded, international Arabic newspaper, he could be a 'somebody.'

Mum continued to be a housewife. She hadn't gone to university and she believed that by giving all her time and undivided attention to her husband and children she was being a good Muslim woman.

I had different aspirations for myself. I was the top student every year during Primary School, I continued to be a teacher's pet and I passed my II+ exam. From there I got into a Grammar School. I was determined that I would be one of these modern Muslim women who would get married but have a career too.

I could be an architect, a scientist, a teacher—my chosen career changed each year. I would go to SOAS, Imperial College or Goldsmith's like all the *amus*' older sons and daughters.

Baba's new job meant more money and more money meant Baba's dream could finally come true. He bought a respectable three-bedroom house in North West London. Our idyllic British-Egyptian family was complete—Mum, Baba, four children, a house with respectable neighbours and lots of *amus* living nearby.

London > Gulf

I was in Year Nine when Baba started to casually drop the names of various Arab Gulf countries into conversations. We would be sitting together in the living room and while my siblings watched TV, I would listen to what my parents were saying. So-and-so got a job in Qatar and is now earning £3,000 a month tax-free. So-and-so moved to Dubai and the children can now speak Arabic fluently. What I didn't realise was that Baba was cleverly planting the idea of looking for a job in the Gulf into Mum's head.

It was only a few months later when Baba dropped a bombshell.

"I've received an offer for my dream job! I'll be a television producer in the Gulf. I'll go for a three-month trial and if I like it you'll move out there to join me."

The news dropped on us like a ton of bricks.

"Why? We've only just got our own house." Mum asked confused. "What's wrong with our life here?"

"When a good opportunity like this comes, it's by the grace of Allah. I'd be a fool to let this opportunity go," Baba replied. "And think of the future. Soon Ahmed and Saffa will become teenagers. Teenage crime is increasing in this country. We'll be living in an Islamic country. It'll be better and safer for the children. Away from bullying, stabbings and drugs."

He didn't ask any of us what we thought about it.

The idea of living in the Gulf wasn't horrendous. I didn't know much about life there, except that the men all wore long white shirt dresses called *thowbs* with Arab headdresses called *ghutra* and *shemaagh*, and their women dressed head-to-toe in black. I saw them in Edgware Road and Knightsbridge, filling their shopping trolleys with five of each item. I knew they were rich.

A month later, one of the *amu*s picked Baba up and drove him to Heathrow Airport. There were no smartphones in 2003. We couldn't Skype or FaceTime him. He called Mum once a week on a Friday—the weekend in the Gulf was Thursday and Friday—and my siblings and I got a few seconds each to say hello before his phone card ran out.

Another month later and Baba informed Mum that things were going well. He would never get the salary and additional benefits he was getting back in England. He had a tax-free salary and monthly allowances for rent, utility bills, and even private school fees.

"It's a huge move," Mum told me one day. She didn't sound too thrilled about it. "He wants us to pack up our whole lives and leave England behind forever. We'll live there for four years until Baba saves enough money to buy a house in Cairo and then he wants us to spend the rest of our lives in Egypt."

I nearly choked on my orange squash. "I don't want to live

in Egypt forever! I can barely stand it when we go there for the summer holidays!"

"It's not up to us, darling. It's up to Baba. Everything is up to Baba."

I was given one month to say goodbye to my friends, teachers, the *amu*s and their families.

Faima, my best friend, cried on my last day at school. My form tutor, Mrs Wilkinson, presented me with a giant, handmade card that everybody in my form had signed. I promised Faima we would write to each other and send emails (in the early 2000s dial-up Internet was starting to become a feature in everyone's household).

Before I knew it, Mum, Ahmed, Saffa, little Abdullah and I were sat on a plane bound for the Gulf.

It felt like I had landed on a different planet. The country looked just how it did on the news reports I had seen back in London with its low-rise beige buildings, tall palm trees lining the streets, stretches of rubbly sand and huge roundabouts.

I found out very quickly that there wasn't much to do. The country had three shopping malls and two cinemas. That was it for entertainment.

Most of the Gulf nationals, known in Arabic as *khaleeji*s, were rich thanks to oil wealth, and they went shopping for fun. Normal folk like us didn't have an endless stream of money to go shopping. So we would walk around the shopping mall and sometimes have a meal out.

The flat Baba rented was gigantic. I'd never seen a flat that big. It was bigger than my aunties' and uncles' flats in Egypt and even bigger than our house in London! Saffa and I would be sharing a bedroom two times the size of our previous one.

We arrived in June, just as the schools were breaking up for the summer holidays, so Baba enrolled us into a school for the next academic year, which would start in mid-September. The summer holidays were longer in the Gulf because it was just too hot to be at school in July.

The first summer was unbearable. We stayed at home lying comatose on the sofas with the flappers on the air conditioning units pointed directly at us as the temperature climbed to 50 degrees Celsius.

"It's like we've come to hell," Mum said, sitting with her head tilted back on the backrest.

As well as it being hot and humid, it was incredibly boring. Baba would be at work until 5pm from Saturday to Wednesday and he would take us out once a week on a Friday. I hadn't been able to bring all of my books with me and when Baba took me to Al Jarir Bookstore I wanted to cry. The only English books they had were classics and I'd read all of those at school.

I went to the bookstore's small magazine section. They sold a few British magazines like *Woman's Weekly* and *Best*, stuff Mum read back in London. I flicked through the pages and saw that any pictures of women who had exposed arms, bellies or legs had been coloured in with a black marker. I wondered whose job it was to do this. I checked the contents page at the beginning of the magazine and discovered that any pages that talked about sex had been removed.

*

Baba was pretty strict in London, but soon after our move to the Gulf we noticed a change in him. He had thrown away all of his Arabic music tapes. I had grown up listening to the famous Lebanese singer Fairouz and the infamous Egyptian singer Umm Kulthum. Baba would play their tapes in the car. It felt like an important part of my childhood had been thrown away.

There were Egyptian *amus* here too, but they were different. They had big beards and no moustaches, and they wore trousers that were too short for them. These were all physical signs that they were *salafis*, a sect of Muslims that were extreme in their interpretation of Islam.

Baba started inviting these *amus* over to our flat two evenings a week for *halaqas* and Mum was expected to cook dinners for them like she had done in London. Mum hadn't minded it in London because she was friends with the *amus'* wives, and the *amus* would bring boxes of chocolates for her as a thank you.

Although she wasn't allowed to see or speak to them, even in London, when they left they would always call out "*shukran um Ahmed,*" which means "Thank you mother of Ahmed." (In Arab culture, married women are called 'mother of' as a sign of respect) to let her know that they were grateful.

There were no boxes of chocolates here and no thank yous. Baba became obsessed with hiding not only Mum, but even me and nine-year-old Saffa. He put up a thick, red curtain, which he drew across the corridor and living room so that we would stay out of sight. Sometimes, Saffa and I would creep up to the curtain to eavesdrop, and Baba would suddenly barge through the curtain and hiss, "*eyb*, go back to your bedrooms!"

We all felt it. Baba was changing. Had he become a *salafi* like the Egyptian *amus*?

The next day I was back in Caffé Nero with Sophie. She was wearing red lipstick that matched mine.

"I just love the fact you wear red lipstick every day," Sophie said, settling into her chair. "Don't you think a bit of red lipstick dresses up any outfit?"

"It does and you look beautiful," I said.

"Were you okay after yesterday's meeting?"

"Oh yes, don't you worry about me. I'll be fine," I reassured her.

I decided not to divulge the fact that the evening before I had been quietly mourning my childhood and listening to Fairouz on YouTube. I didn't want her thinking that talking about my life would affect me psychologically in any way. If anything, talking to Sophie was like the therapy I had never had.

Sophie smiled. "Shall we pick up from where we left off?"

She switched on her voice recorder.

Faisal

"Bring your *hijab* down and cover your chest. It's useless tied around your neck."

Baba walked over to where I was standing in the hallway and yanked the little knot I had made with the two ends of my headscarf behind my neck.

"But my school shirt covers my chest," I protested.

"No, this is not proper *hijab*. Proper *hijab* should be worn so that it covers your chest."

Baba and I stood face-to-face as he put his large brown hands with his spindly fingers around my neck and undid the knotted fabric.

As soon as he had dropped me, Ahmed and Saffa off outside the school gates and was out of sight, I tied the ends of my *hijab* around my neck again.

"If he finds out you're gonna get in trouble," Ahmed warned.

"How's he gonna find out? Are you gonna tell him?" I asked him daringly.

"Come on let's go, we're gonna be late," Ahmed said shaking his head, and he hurried towards the boys' entrance.

Tying my *hijab* around my neck was important. It was a tiny act of defiance in the face of Baba who was becoming stricter by the day.

Baba had enrolled us into a private international school that wasn't very international as it was attended mainly by *khaleeji* kids a.k.a people from the Gulf.

Classes were segregated—all schools in the country were segregated except for the American schools—but boys and girls shared the same building, so I got to see the boys sometimes as I moved from class to class. I was in Year 10, Ahmed was in Year 7 and Saffa was in Year 5, so she was in a separate building for the Primary School children.

The rules around being friends with boys had changed since we left London. Saffa and I didn't make friends with the new *amu*s' sons and Ahmed didn't make friends with their daughters. Saffa and I were explicitly forbidden by Baba from having male friendships. Ahmed had not been given the same warning.

In London the rules were the same for all of us but now that we were in the Gulf, Baba had become like every other Arab father who made separate rules for his daughters and sons.

"Things are different here, Sara," Baba told me during the car ride to school one morning. "Here, each girl has to mind her reputation. The reputation of a girl is the reputation of her family. Only bad girls mix with boys here. And don't forget the *hadith*, the saying of the Prophet Muhammed, peace be upon him, that when a man and a woman are alone, the devil is the third-party."

"But I'm not a woman yet," I replied.

"You went through puberty. In Islam this means you're a woman. Allah will hold you accountable now for your deeds."

"But how come you let me be friends with the *amus*' sons in London?"

"I told you, things are different here and anyway, you were young in London."

"Does that mean you would have stopped me being friends with *amu* Khairy's sons and *amu* Yousry's sons once I had turned fifteen in London?"

"Don't try to act clever with me, Sara! In London life is different. The people here in the Arab world aren't used to speaking to the opposite sex. Just trust me on this. I know how people think here."

I missed the fun I had hanging out with the *amus*' sons in London, but when I observed the Gulf boys in school, they didn't look like they were worth breaking Baba's new rules for anyway.

Walking through the school corridor to my next lesson, I observed one *khaleeji* boy (who had a bowl haircut and a light moustache) flatten his face against the wall every time a girl walked past him, taking quick glimpses to make sure the girl had completely gone before he unflattened himself and resumed walking.

Our Arabic teacher, Miss Reema, came from Jordan and she didn't fit the stereotype of an Arabic teacher at all. Arabic teachers usually wore long, thick, ankle-length overcoats called *jilbabs*, big headscarves that were tightly pinned under the chin, and no make-up. They were the biggest prudes.

But Miss Reema was different. She was in her late 20s, and she wore lots of makeup, a tiny headscarf tucked into her blouse and skinny jeans. You don't understand how much of a big deal it is for an Arabic teacher to wear jeans! Most Arabic teachers taught girls that wearing trousers was *haram*. Any form of clothing that showed the outline of your legs was *haram*.

Miss Reema was more like a big sister. She always came into class smelling of cigarettes and she loved gossiping about the boys since she taught them Arabic and Islamic Studies too.

At the end of Arabic lesson one day, she came over to where I sat at my desk and said, "You know Faisal from Year 9? He told me he likes you."

I had seen Faisal around the school several times. I knew who he was because he hung out with two boys called Saud and Rayyan, who were accused by everyone of being gay. Saud and Rayyan looked and behaved effeminately, and I think that was why the students, both the boys and the girls, believed they were gay. Rumours were rife in the school about his two friends being bummed by the older boys in the toilets.

The Gulf was strange. If you were the guy on top you weren't considered gay, but if you were the guy receiving, you were. Having grown up in London I had no issues with gay people even though Baba kept telling me how *haram* it was to be homosexual. Saud and Rayyan were ostracised by everybody at school, and because Faisal was friends with them, he was side-lined by the other boys too.

I had never given Faisal a second glance, until one day, we crossed paths in the corridor, and he smiled at me. He was the year below me, but you could have easily thought he was eighteen with his thick black moustache and goatee. He had straight, shoulder-length, black hair. Faisal was cute.

"You know if you want to talk to him, you could meet in my office at lunchtime. I won't tell anyone," Miss Reema suggested.

I really missed the fun and banter I had with *amus'* sons in London.

I'm sure I can have a secret guy friend here at school and no one will find out, I thought to myself.

So I told Miss Reema I was up for meeting Faisal in her office the next day at lunchtime.

When I turned up at her office the next day I was disappointed that Faisal's mates Saud and Rayyan had tagged along. I could tell that Faisal was struggling to talk to me. Every time he asked me a question about myself it was immediately followed by serious amounts of blushing. It seemed like he had never had an actual conversation with a girl before.

Faisal ordered McDonalds for all of us and his chauffer dropped it off at the school gates. This is one thing I did love about the Gulf. It was perfectly acceptable to have your family chauffeur pick up your lunch from a restaurant of your choosing and drop it off at school. We ate the McDonalds as the boys did impersonations of our teachers, making me laugh so hard that I got stitches.

I didn't really hear from my friends back in London but I was getting on great with the Gulf girls at school, although when they spoke about things like shopping for designer bags or the couture dresses they wore to weddings I felt a little left out.

I had become particularly close to one girl in the year below me, Muneera. Her father was an ambassador and even though she was a Gulfie she had spent most of her life living in London. She had moved back two years ago and was the one person at school who could relate to the culture shock I was currently experiencing.

I told Muneera about my lunch 'date.'

"Sara, if you get caught mixing with male students you'll be in big trouble with the headmistress," Muneera warned me, "It's not worth it. You're not in London anymore. Boys and girls here don't mix freely, not even as friends. It's frowned upon culturally. The rare time a Gulf girl talks to a guy and gets caught, if she isn't beaten up and grounded for life by her family, she is called a *gahba*."

"What's a *gahba*?" I asked.

"It's like the Egyptian word *sharmootah*. It means slut."

"You're worrying too much Muneera," I said. "Miss Reema has my back. It'll be fine."

"I'm just looking out for you Sara. I don't want to see you get in trouble," Muneera said quietly and we ended our conversation as we entered the classroom.

But I was wrong. Miss Reema pulled me aside after an Arabic lesson.

"Sara, I need to talk to you. I don't think you should come to my office at lunchtime anymore to hang out with the boys. One of the girls in Year 9 spotted you through my office window and rumours have started to fly around. This could be bad for your reputation. If it gets back to your father, he won't be happy."

"But it was your idea! You told me about Faisal."

"I know and I was wrong," Miss Reema said, avoiding eye contact with me. "You need to end it."

"Fine," I said.

Miss Reema sighed relieved. She smiled at me, pinched

my cheek like I was a little kid and then walked out of the classroom.

I had no intention of not spending time with my new friends.

Clandestine Meetings

I allowed a week to slide by without meeting up with the boys before suggesting to Faisal over Windows Live Messenger that we find a quiet spot in the school to carry on hanging out during lunchtime. This time without Miss Reema or Saud and Rayyan. It was Faisal I was interested in talking to. As well as being cute, he was incredibly nice and softly spoken, not like the British Egyptian boys who were only up for a laugh and pulling a prank.

There was a small classroom in the corner of the first floor that nobody went to. We sat huddled together in the corner and without Saud and Rayyan, our conversation took a serious turn.

"Do you like it here?" Faisal asked.

I sighed. "It's. . . different. My dad is much stricter here and it's going to take me a minute to adjust. Is your dad strict?"

Faisal looked at the floor. "My dad's an alcoholic and he thinks I'm gay because I hang out with Saud and Rayyan. He thinks they're too feminine. No matter how many times I tell him I'm not gay, he doesn't listen."

"That sounds awful," I said, wrapping one arm around him.

"He whips me and he says he's going to beat the homosexuality out of me."

I gasped. "Doesn't anyone stand up for you?"

Faisal shook his head. "He doesn't bother my older brother Hamad. He's a star footballer. My dad used to be a professional football player. Everyday he says how proud he is of Hamad for being a proper man and I'm nothing but a disappointment."

My heart broke so much for him that I couldn't help but hug him tight. At first he was tense but then he relaxed into me and we stayed like that for what felt like hours.

"I really enjoy talking to you," Faisal said as we got ready to leave the classroom—I always left first and he left a few minutes afterwards to avoid suspicion. "Can I have your mobile number?"

"I'm not allowed to have a mobile phone," I confessed. It was true. Baba said there was no reason for me to have one. "But I can call you from our landline at home?"

I waved him goodbye as he waited in the classroom. It was a risky alternative. There was no saying what Baba might do if he caught me talking to a boy on the phone after he had explicitly forbidden it.

I figured out that there were only two instances during which it would be safe for me to take the cordless landline telephone into the bedroom I shared with Saffa.

One: When he was out in the evening at one of the *amus'* houses.

Two: When he went to pray at the mosque.

He always took an hour at the mosque when it came to *ishaa,* the last prayer of the day. Muslims pray five times a day: *fajr* at dawn, *dhuhr* when the sun is at its highest point, *asr* when the sun starts to dip in the sky, *maghrib* when the sun sets and finally *ishaa* when night has fallen.

Baba would drag Ahmed along with him, telling him, "You're not a man if you don't pray at the mosque."

Abdullah was only five and too young to understand anything if he walked in on me talking on the phone to a boy. I wasn't concerned about Saffa or Ahmed. We always had each other's backs, but sometimes Mum was an issue.

I felt sorry for her because she was powerless when it came to Baba. She did her best to keep our secrets; she would swear on Allah's name that she wouldn't tell. But when Baba was suspicious and wanted to find out something, he would resort to threatening divorce and said he'd send her back to England, telling her that he would keep us kids and that she would never see us again, so she would eventually cave in. He played on the country's laws, which stated that it was a woman's legal duty to obey her husband.

Since our move to the Gulf, Mum and Baba had started to fight more often. Even though our luxurious and spacious flat was a palace compared to the poky council flat in Pimlico, when my parents shouted at each other there was nowhere my siblings and I could escape to. Hanging outside our block of flats, when it was 40 degrees and as humid as a sauna, was not an option.

Mum didn't know how to drive and in this new country—apart from the orange and white taxis with their poor air conditioning—there was no public transport. She was effectively a prisoner in her own home and she depended on Baba for everything.

Baba invited the new *amu*s along with their wives and

children over to our place several times for tea, but their wives were not like the aunties in London. They didn't speak much English and Mum couldn't speak much Arabic. She tried hard to make conversation with them in broken Arabic, interjections of English and hand gestures, but most of the time the aunties didn't understand her. Eventually she gave up.

*

One evening, Baba announced that he was going to visit a friend, so I waited for half an hour after he had gone, making sure Mum and my siblings were sat together in our living room, fully engrossed in *Holby City*. I quietly took the cordless telephone to my bedroom. Gently closing the door behind me, I opened the noisy air-conditioning unit and sat in a corner, hoping that the rackety sound of the motors would muffle my voice.

I was so nervous that when I dialled Faisal's number, I almost hoped he wouldn't pick up. But after a few rings he answered.

"Hello?"

"Hey Faisal, it's me, Sara."

"You did it, you called! Is your dad at home?"

Faisal was whispering into the phone as if he was worried someone from my side would overhear his voice.

"No, no, he went out, and I waited to make sure he was gone before calling you. How's things at home now?"

"I'm just trying to stay out of my dad's way. I stay upstairs in my room unless I'm called down by my mum to eat. If she allowed me to eat in my room I wouldn't even come down for that, because we all sit at the dining table and eat together, and that's when my dad starts on me."

"Same here. We eat our dinner together as a family, except we eat in silence. Has he hit you this week?"

"It's been a few days since the last beating. He only hits me when he's drunk and he hasn't been drunk so far this week. If my mum tries to stop him he starts hitting her too."

"Can't you and your mum pack your things and go to her family?"

"We can't. Her parents died when I was a young child, and she refuses to tell my aunties and uncles what's going on. In our culture it's *eyb* to tell anyone, not even your relatives, that your husband does something that is considered shameful like drinking. Here, they believe that you should cover up your family's sins, not expose them to other people."

"What about the police? Social services?"

"This isn't London. Over here the police will just make my dad sign a form promising never to do it again and social services will encourage my mum to stay with my dad and try work things out. It's still considered shameful for a woman to get divorced here. If my mum pushes for a divorce, our society will blame her. They'll say she must have done something to make her husband hit her. We're trapped Sara."

It dawned on me that my own mother was trapped too, but had the opposite problem. Instead of being unable to get divorced, Mum lived under the constant threat of being divorced by Baba and losing her children forever.

*

Faisal and I started to meet up regularly at break times. We would find excuses to leave in the middle of class just to exchange a stolen hello in the corridor. I had never liked a boy like this in the UK. Thinking about it, I didn't ever spend enough time alone with a boy to develop any feelings.

Whenever I hung out with the *amu*s' sons, we were always in a big group, and my brother Ahmed was always there. But now whenever I saw Faisal, my heart skipped a beat.

"I think I like you," I told him at the end of one of our clandestine meetings.

"I like you too," he said back.

Forbidden Love

"Sara, Mrs Klaxon wants to see you in her office," my form tutor Miss Brown told me after taking the register one morning. I had never been called to see the deputy headmistress before.

"Do you know why?" I asked.

"No idea," she answered before dashing out of the classroom to deliver her first history lesson of the day.

I excused myself and headed downstairs to Mrs Klaxon's office. She was a New Zealander in her 50s with dyed blonde hair cut in a symmetrical bob that fell just below her ears. She wore half-moon glasses perched midway on her nose, and the same dangly, gold, bauble earrings every day. Whenever she talked, she would peer down at you over her glasses, and her hair and earrings would swing from side to side.

"Hello Sara!" she greeted me warmly. "Please come and have a seat beside me." She motioned to the spare armchair next to hers. I sat down. "How are you settling into school and your new home? I know you only moved here from the UK last summer."

"I'm loving it," I lied.

"Sara, it's come to my attention that you've not been going outdoors during break and lunchtime like the other students," she said.

Shit. She knew.

"You have to understand that while it may be ordinary to mix with the opposite sex in other countries, it's not acceptable here. We need to respect the customs and traditions of this country."

I felt myself go hot under the collar. I didn't respond. I honestly didn't know what to say.

"Please leave Faisal alone. You're one of our eldest and brightest students, and the younger girls look up to you as a role model. If they see you mixing with boys, they might think that this is acceptable behaviour for them too. Can we come to an agreement on this?" she asked.

I nodded, but I had no intention of following through. Faisal and I had to keep seeing each other. We couldn't see each other outside school, so this was the only place we had to meet.

*

My secret relationship with Faisal lasted three months before I got caught calling him. One day, Baba came home from work with a wad of papers in one hand, his briefcase in the other. I was watching TV in the living room with Saffa and Ahmed.

"Come into the next room, Sara, I need to talk to you," Baba said. He looked gravely serious.

Saffa and Ahmed gave me sympathetic glances. We all knew I was in trouble.

Thinking it might be something to do with my latest school

report, where my grades had fallen from As to Bs and Cs, I thought I was in for a lecture about not studying hard enough. Egyptian fathers expected nothing less than straight As.

I followed him into Ahmed and Abdullah's bedroom, which doubled up as a place where we could chill when the *amus* were over. Baba sat on the small two-seater sofa in the corner of the room, and I sat across from him on Abdullah's bed.

"I noticed the phone bill has gone up by three times the usual amount," Baba said, waving the wad of papers with rows and rows of numbers. "Do you know anything about this?"

Shit!

I thought I had been clever by making the phone calls when he wasn't around, but I had completely forgotten about the phone bills, which gave an itemised record of every outgoing call.

"No," I said, looking him straight in the eye.

"Come over here," Baba ordered. I slowly stood up and walked to the side of the sofa, my legs shaking. "Look at this number." He jabbed Faisal's mobile number with his forefinger. "It appears over and over again. Have you been calling this number?"

I felt my heart in my throat, knowing I was moments away from being caught out.

"Oh! That's Muneera's number," I lied.

"No. This is not Muneera's number. I called it."

My hands started to tremble and my head felt so hot that I thought it might implode. I went back and sat quietly on Abdullah's bed, awaiting my sentence.

"Did I not tell you when we moved here that you're forbidden from talking to boys?" he growled.

I stayed silent.

"You didn't learn your lesson. So there will be no phone and no Internet," he said.

I waited for more but Baba left the room furious, muttering things in Arabic under his breath. *This* time I'd avoided a beating.

As soon as Baba went to pray *ishaa* that evening, Mum grabbed me by the arm, ushered me into her bedroom and locked the door behind us.

"Baba told me what happened. Calling boys Sara! Are you trying to get yourself beaten up?" she asked, shaking her head in disbelief.

"It's just a friend from school Mum, I promise!"

"Baba told you specifically that you can't be friends with boys in this country."

"So, am I not going to talk to a boy until I get married?"

"Look, I'm sure we aren't going to live here forever. When we move to Egypt I'm sure the rules will relax again as people are not as strict there."

"Oh great, how exciting is that? Speaking to boys in Egypt— lucky me."

"Cut the sarcasm please. Do what Baba says and don't do stupid things that will get you in trouble, because then I get in trouble too!"

"What do you mean?"

"Every time one of you kids do something wrong, he takes it out on me."

Mum suddenly went silent and looked at the floor.

"What does he do?"

"Nothing." Mum shook her head. "It's nothing for you to worry about."

I held her hand and squeezed it gently. "Please tell me. What does he do?"

"You're too young to understand the things that happen between adults," Mum said quietly.

"I'm going to be sixteen in three months. I'm not a baby. Mum, tell me," I pleaded.

"Do you really want to know? Okay, every time your father is angry and you lot are asleep, he hurts me. He pulls my hair and shoves me against the wall and tells me that I'm a terrible wife and mother and that he should get rid of me, and then he forces himself—" Mum shook her head and started to cry. She rolled her free hand into a fist, putting it under her nose to try and control her sobs.

I froze. I knew what she was going to say. I felt like I was going to throw up. I pulled her towards me and held her tight.

What was I going to do? I couldn't bear the thought of my life without Faisal in it. But what if Baba caught me again? What would he do to Mum? I would have to be more cautious. I wasn't ready to give up Faisal just yet.

*

At school, Faisal and I continued our secret meetings whenever we got the opportunity. But the next day, at break time, Faisal came to our meeting spot with his head almost clean shaven and black and blue bruises under both eyes.

"What happened?" I gasped. "Did your dad do this to you?"

He nodded. "He was drunk last night and accused me again

of sleeping with older men. He told me if I didn't cut my long hair he would do it himself. When I refused he beat me with a stick and took an electric razor to my head."

I wrapped my arms around him. I'd been taught by Baba that touching a male who wasn't my relative was *haram* but I didn't care. Faisal needed someone to comfort him.

"You know you actually look really handsome with short hair," I said, trying my best to cheer him up.

"Thank you, but I liked it how it was."

"Look, why don't you tell your dad about me and say I'm your girlfriend?"

"I don't think he'll believe me."

"I'll talk to him. I'm sure he'll leave you alone once he has actual evidence that you're attracted to girls."

"I'll think about it," Faisal said. He tried to smile but ended up wincing instead.

To be honest, I was frightened of talking to his father. A man who beats his son black and blue wasn't someone I wanted to face. I'd never spoken to a grown Gulf man, and they seemed scarier than Baba.

Egypt

I'd been dreading the last day of summer term. I knew Faisal and I would be apart for three whole months! And even worse, I'd be stuck in Egypt.

Baba called it a holiday, but for Mum, my siblings and I, going to Cairo was less of a holiday and more of an ordeal. The streets were heavily polluted with litter. When you got out of a car you had to mind where you put your foot in case you stood in a heap of rubbish or a stream of sewage. There were no car lanes; vehicles surged in hordes across the roads, and most of them didn't have air conditioning. If you got stuck in traffic, in a hot taxi, you'd need the windows wound all the way down and you'd be gasping for air. If you wiped your face with a tissue it would turn black from the particles of smoke that had embedded themselves in your skin.

Females had to deal with men catcalling and wolf-whistling, and there were always random street fights breaking out.

In the flat Baba owned next door to his sister, the electricity and water would get cut off on a daily basis. We didn't do any of the fun touristy things. We spent most of our so-called holiday at Baba's relatives' houses trying to make small talk in the little Arabic we knew, batting away incessant flies.

We couldn't even take refuge in the delicious food, because we always ended up with at least one case of food poisoning, and it wasn't like the food poisoning you got in the UK. Whatever strain of bacteria they had in Egypt was merciless, leaving you either shooting projectile vomit out of one end and diarrhoea out the other end simultaneously, or it would have you doubled up on the floor crying from excruciating gut pain.

"I'll try to go to an Internet café with Ahmed and send you an email, or I'll use my cousins' computer when I get the chance," I reassured Faisal on the last day at school.

We had met in our secret spot in the small, abandoned classroom one last time before the summer holidays began.

"I'll miss you," I told Faisal, standing up on my tippy toes so that I could wrap my arms around his neck.

"I'll miss you too," he said, holding me tight.

"I think I love you." I don't know where the words came from and I'm not sure I even knew what love was. The words just tumbled out of my mouth.

"I love you too."

I looked at him and he looked at me and we planted a kiss on each other's lips. It was nothing passionate or prolonged, just a peck, but it made us blush. My heart fluttered like a bird flapping about in a cage.

"When we've both graduated from high school I'm going to persuade my parents to let me marry you," he said.

"I'd love that!" And at the time I meant it.

Home was depressing. I had many sleepless nights worrying that my parents were on the brink of a divorce and that our family was at risk of being broken up, I felt like being a high school bride was a perfectly acceptable idea. The Gulf girls did it; they got married as soon as they finished high school, so why couldn't I? Faisal and I could grow into adulthood together and take care of one another. Plus, his family was rich, so we wouldn't have to worry about money.

We said our goodbyes and I left the classroom first.

On the ride home with Baba after school, Ahmed wasn't his usual jokey self. He sulked the whole way home.

"You alright, Ahmed?" I asked as we walked up the stairs to our flat on the first floor. He didn't answer. "Was it someone at school? Did someone say or do something to you?"

He scowled and turned his face away from mine. I couldn't think of anything I might have said or done to make him so upset. So I brushed it off and told myself he was just being a hormonal, prepubescent boy.

Later that evening, when Baba and Ahmed had gone to pray at the mosque, Mum called me to her bedroom and shut the door behind us.

"Ahmed is really upset. He said one of his classmates told him after school that he saw you kissing a boy. Is this true?"

"No!" I exclaimed. I couldn't let this get to Baba. "I swear to God it's not true. The boys at school love spreading false rumours about the girls."

"You had better be telling the truth," Mum hissed. "I'll tell Ahmed the boys at school are just making trouble and to forget about it. I doubt he'll say anything to Baba and you better hope Baba doesn't hear it from anybody else."

"I promise you, it's all lies," I said, looking her straight in the eye, trying to keep my facial expression as blank as possible.

Mum sighed. "I only just spoke to you about following Baba's rules a few weeks ago. I hope for both our sakes that you're telling the truth."

*

A few days later, we were sat in economy class on an aeroplane bound for Egypt. I missed Faisal like crazy, and couldn't wait to go to my aunt's house so that I could send him an email.

Oh, how I hated flying to Egypt. The air stewardesses were lazy and rude, and would tut when you asked them just for a cup of water. Women changed their babies' dirty nappies on their laps and left the poo-filled nappies in the little elastic net at the back of the seat in front of them, stinking up the entire aisle. Children climbed all over the seats. I turned around several times to give the kids behind me death stares when they kicked my chair. It felt like my nightmare holiday had already begun.

When we landed in the airport and finally got through customs and baggage collection, we were greeted at the main entrance by Baba's two younger brothers and his brother-in-law. After having lived for almost a year in the constant sweaty sauna that is the Gulf, Egypt's dry heat was a welcome surprise. The flies were still annoying though. There were no flies in the Gulf, probably because it was too hot for anything to survive.

I knew that this so-called holiday was cursed when my youngest uncle was texting while driving, then dropped his phone under his legs and proceeded to try and pick it up with one hand while holding the steering wheel with the other. The car took a sharp swerve across the highway and we all screamed as we thought he'd lost control of the car. He panicked and managed to regain control, just as I thought we might veer off into the River Nile.

A couple of days later, while Baba was taking a shower in our dusty Cairo flat, I found our return air tickets. They were poking out of his little black travel bag which he had left on the dining table.

All the furniture in our flat was the classic wooden furniture fashioned in 17th-century French style. You would find the exact same style of furniture in every Egyptian household. I liked the woody smell of the hardback chairs in the living room and the sounds the crystals of the chandelier made when they knocked together as the breeze came through the open balcony.

Baba had told us that we were only going to be here for three weeks, and when I looked at the return date, I discovered that he'd lied. We were going to be here for double that amount of time!

I went to Mum, who was sipping her morning cup of coffee on the balcony, and told her what I'd found.

"Did you know about this?" I asked her, furious that I was going to have to bear this country for over a month.

"I didn't but I'm honestly not surprised. It's just another one of his lies," she replied nonchalantly as she ate a digestive biscuit.

"Why aren't you as angry as I am?" I demanded.

"I'm tired," Mum said. "I carry on for the sake of you children. I want you all to have a good education and go to university. I don't want to jeopardise your futures by making unnecessary trouble with your father. You need to learn how to pick your battles."

I sat across from her silently on a brown leather pouffe, and peered down at the streets below; the caretaker's wife was sitting on the steps of the building's entrance, her head cradled in her hand. She was watching the people walk by, a look of misery etched into her face. The caretaker might have been much poorer than Baba, but I doubted Baba's attitude towards women was any different to the caretaker's.

Love Sick

We were three weeks into our stay and I had managed a weekly email to Faisal on my cousins' computer. I missed him so much.

I thought I'd escaped the danger of food poisoning as we'd eaten at a variety of restaurants without any ill effects. I became confident that the second half of our holiday in Egypt would pass food poisoning free. I was so confident that when we went to a fried chicken restaurant, I ate as much coleslaw from their open salad bar as I could stomach.

"Give us some of yours," Ahmed said, trying to take my salad bowl away from me.

"Hey!" I snapped, pulling the bowl back. "Get your own!"

A few hours later, I was sat on the toilet in our flat, a plastic bowl on my lap to catch the vomit. At least this time the vomit and diarrhoea weren't happening simultaneously.

"That'll teach you for being a greedy madam and not sharing with your brother," Mum told me, handing me an anti-sickness tablet.

But 24 hours later, I was still so ill that I felt like the entire contents of my body had spilled out. The colon spasms were so bad that I had to crawl to the toilet.

Mum and Baba thought I was being a drama queen until I started to become delirious. I wan't fully aware of myself or my surroundings and I spent the next two days in a daze between the hard mattress of my old-fashioned bed and the bathroom, trailing watery poo behind me on the floor. At this point, Mum realised that this was not an ordinary bout of food poisoning.

"We're going to have to take her to a hospital," she told Baba.

She ran a warm bath and helped me take off my clothes and step into the bathtub, where she scrubbed my body like a young child. Baba stood in the doorway and I was so out of it that I didn't care that he could see me naked.

With our spending money for the holiday being almost double in value when you converted it from Gulf currency to Egyptian pounds, we expected Baba to take us to a private hospital. Instead, he took us to a charity medical dispensary ran by people he knew.

The car journey to the dispensary felt like it took forever as I laid my tired head against Mum's shoulder. It turned out that the dispensary had only been a ten minute car ride away, but it felt like hours.

As soon as we got to the dispensary, a young male nurse with a neatly-groomed, black beard helped me onto a wheelchair: the beige canvas fabric of the seat was frayed and grubby. Minutes later I was laid down on an uncomfortable and narrow hospital bed, hooked up to clear bags of saline, with Mum sat beside me, peering anxiously down into my face as I slipped in and out of consciousness.

The doctor was a middle-aged man with a beard that rivalled Father Christmas and he stood to the side of my bed to talk with Baba.

Everyone looked so serious that I wondered if I was dying. I also wondered why I'd been brought to this poor person's hospital, with its brown tiles that reminded me of the hospitals I'd seen in documentaries about Victorian England.

"How are you feeling?" Baba asked.

"*Alhamdulillah*, all praise and thanks to God," I whispered. I felt so weak.

"You know, when Allah loves His servant He gives them a test to see how strong their faith is. Consider this a test from Allah," Baba said.

I had no physical or mental strength to reply, so I just nodded my head, which felt heavy with exhaustion.

Once the fluid in the IV had finished dripping, Mum helped me go to the toilet to give a stool sample.

"I'm not doing it in here!" I cried.

Not only did this single cubicle have no lock on the door, but there were old poo stains on the toilet bowl and the floor around it, and no toilet paper to clean myself with.

"Stop behaving like a toddler, Sara!" Mum said, crossly. "There are things in life you have to do even if you don't like it, and this is one of them!"

But I couldn't bring myself to go anywhere near that filthy toilet, so in the end she gave up and we went back to the room.

"I can't believe you brought us here," Mum said furiously to Baba, no longer trying to hide her anger, and not caring that the doctor probably understood some English. "Get us out of here and take us to a private hospital that is clean."

On the car ride back to the flat he promised Mum he would take us to a private hospital first thing the next morning.

Back in the flat, the only thing I managed to ingest was 7Up. Seems that all those Egyptian aunties who said 7Up fixed a dodgy tummy were right.

The next morning Baba took us to a shiny, new clinic, and I finally managed to give a stool sample in the clean, polished, white, ceramic bathroom. Since Baba had slipped the receptionist at the clinic some extra cash, he got the test results ready for us within a couple hours and I got my diagnosis.

I had amoebic dysentery. A parasite had found its way into my intestines, and I could have literally pooed myself to death, as it causes you to lose all your fluids through intense diarrhoea. I had probably got it from the coleslaw in the fried chicken restaurant.

"Do you realise this is a Victorian illness?" Mum asked Baba as they stood over me in the living room of our flat.

I was sat on the floor, leaning over a plastic bowl, trying to keep down the strong antibiotics the private hospital had supplied me with. They left a pungent taste on my tongue and I struggled to swallow them without bringing them back up. In the end, the only way I could keep them down was by taking them crushed in a teaspoon of strawberry jam.

Over the next couple of days my health drastically improved. The diarrhoea and vomiting lessened until they both stopped and I managed to keep down the chicken and onion soup that my aunt next door kept sending over for me. I felt the strength slowly return to my body. I had lost six kilograms in the space of one week and when I looked at myself in the bathroom mirror, I looked gaunt and frail.

*

There was just over a week to go until our flight back to the Gulf and Baba was spending a lot of time meeting friends and distant cousins, leaving Mum, Saffa, Abdullah and I to languish in our stuffy flat with nothing to do except watch the two satellite channels on the TV that were in English, or read the books we'd brought along with us on the trip. Ahmed was staying at our cousins' house and had decided to remain there for the rest of our holiday.

Mum was still furious with Baba for taking me to the cheap hospital.

"You would never have got sick like that in England," Mum said, as we sat in the living room. My siblings were in their bedrooms. "We have to come up with a plan to run away from the Gulf and go back home even if it means we take off our *hijabs* and pretend to Gran that we're leaving Islam, so that she takes us in."

"But I can't leave the Gulf," I told her.

"Why? There's nothing to keep us there! You can repeat Year 10 back home in the UK if you have to. I thought you wanted to go back?"

Just a few months ago I'd been telling her how much I hated the Gulf and that I would give anything to be able to go back to the UK.

"Mum, I want to tell you a secret," I said. "But you have to promise me not to tell Baba."

"I won't."

"Remember the last day of school when Ahmed's classmate said he saw me kiss a boy? I lied. I did kiss a boy."

Mum gasped. "Sara, you swore to me you hadn't! Why did you lie to me?"

"I'm in love, Mum. His name is Faisal, and as soon as he finishes high school we're going to get married."

"No," Mum said, shaking her head. "You're barely sixteen, you're far too young to think about marriage. You're acting crazy."

"But I love him!" I pleaded. "And I'm going to be with him. Are you going to tell Baba?"

"Don't be stupid. Of course I'm not going to tell Baba," she said. "This conversation ends now."

"Sara, sit down," Baba said, later that evening. He pointed to the sofa, which was positioned directly opposite the hardback armchair he was sat on. "I've decided that you're not coming back to the Gulf with us. I've found a place for you in a private all-girls school and you'll be living here with your Aunt Mona."

"No! You can't leave me here. I hate this country! You can't force me to stay here," I cried, slipping slowly off the sofa on to the floor, where I knelt before him.

"I warned you. I said no relationships with boys before marriage but you disobeyed me again," Baba said. "And you are having a relationship with someone who mixes with gays. Yes, I know all about it. Ahmed told me everything."

"He wants to marry me! You can't force me to do anything. I'll find a way back to Faisal from here. I'll marry him no matter what you say," I shouted.

Baba grabbed me roughly by the arm and pulled me up onto my feet. "*Ya zift, ya bint al kalb!*" 'You piece of shit. You're a daughter of a dog' in Arabic. Then he hit me across the side of my head. "If you want me to forbid you from going to school and keep you locked up, I will."

He brought his face close to mine; his eyes were in front of me, and I could smell his putrid breath. In the corner of my eye, I could see Mum. She was standing in the doorway of their bedroom, trembling with fear.

"Are you going to just stand there and let this happen?" I yelled. "Please, Mum!"

"Mustafa, please!" she said, and she made her way towards us. "Give her a second chance. We can put her in another school."

"You shut up!" Baba shouted. "If I find out that you knew about your daughter's slutty behaviour I'll divorce you and you'll never see your children again."

Mum froze.

"Please, Baba, I swear to Allah I won't speak to Faisal ever again if you let me come back with you. I'll never speak to a boy again," I begged.

Baba let go of my arm and sat down in his armchair once more.

"I'm sorry *ya Sara*," he said, softening his tone, and for a moment I thought he'd changed his mind. "I'm your father and I know what's best for you."

*

A couple of days before my family were due to leave, Baba had still not changed his mind. I sat at the dinner table not touching my food and Baba watched me, a deep frown on his face.

"Please, Sara, eat something," Mum pleaded, and I shook my head.

"You think this is helping you?" Baba yelled.

He stood up, walked over to me, lifted a piece of chicken and tried to force it into my mouth. I spat it out.

"I would rather kill myself than stay here," I hissed before I pushed back my chair and stormed towards the balcony.

A sense of vertigo rushed over me as I peered down at the tops of the cars whizzing past below. I stood right at the edge and closed my eyes.

"*Khalas*! *Enough*! Fine!" Baba said from behind me. "You can come back, but get down from there at once."

I took several steps back, my heart thundering in my ears.

"You will not be going back to the same school," Baba said. "And if I ever catch you having relations with boys again you'll be on the next plane back here."

"Yes, Baba," I said.

Sara—1. Baba—0.

Ahmed

Once we got home, I thought long and hard about my relationship with Faisal. I could continue it in secret, but I knew it would be hard when we weren't going to the same school.

At some point I would mess up along the way, be caught by Baba again and sent on the next plane to Egypt, or, I could make the very tough decision to end things.

Every time I thought about the second option, I would have to rush myself to the bathroom before I burst into tears. I buried my face into a wad of loo roll, trying to muffle out my sobs. I didn't want anyone at home to see or hear me crying and wonder what was up. They all assumed things were already over with Faisal.

For those first few weeks back in the Gulf, I didn't check my email inbox, not even when the coast was clear for me to do so. I needed some time to build up the strength before I sent him an email to tell him I couldn't carry on being his girlfriend anymore.

The events in Egypt still felt too fresh and I knew that if

I saw an email from him now, I would cave in and carry on with our relationship in secret, risking my future.

When we returned after that fateful summer in Egypt, I accepted that my new school may be one of the private Islamic girls' schools run by Wahhabis—followers of the extremely conservative sect of Islam that was endorsed by the governments in the Gulf.

It would be the type of school that was surrounded by high walls to protect, if not blind, the female students from the outside world. Where students would be wearing the *niqab* from the age of twelve, but be able to discard it along with their *hijabs* once they were safely within the inside perimeters of the school. A school where a cast of all female teachers would teach you that it was your absolute duty to obey your brothers, husbands and fathers, and your primary goal in life was to get married and push out babies.

You can imagine my surprise when Baba announced that he was putting Ahmed, Saffa and I in a British school that was co-ed. Instead of moving me further away from the opposite sex I would now be sitting next to them in class just as I had in London. I was confused. Had the events of the summer made Baba see the error of his ways? Was he going to relax and be more like the Baba he was in London?

"You silly girl," Mum said, when I asked her why he had moved me to a co-ed school instead of an Islamic girls' school. "It's cheaper than the last school you went to, that's why Baba chose it."

The night before our first day at the new school, Baba sat me down. "You do not sit next to boys during class, and you will not mix with boys at break time. If I hear from anyone that you have been mixing with boys I'll take you out of school and keep you at home."

The trouble I'd caused over the summer had not been forgotten, but Baba had stopped bringing up my attempt to throw myself over the balcony in every other conversation. I was allowed to use the house phone under supervision, and I kept in touch with my friend Muneera.

"I turn up on the first day of term, and do you know what they've done?" Muneera asked me over the phone.

"No, go on, tell me," I said.

"They've separated the boys and girls into two separate buildings and built a giant concrete wall between them."

I had a feeling this had been down to me.

*

Baba kept a strict eye on how I dressed and behaved in public. He would give me a once-over every morning before we left to go to school. I ditched my big square headscarves for black rectangular scarves called *shaylas* worn by the Gulf girls.

"I don't like these *shaylas*," Baba said. "They don't cover your chest properly."

But I ignored him and eventually he stopped saying anything.

I started to wear make-up. At the beginning it was just a few coats of black mascara, but I soon made the addition of black eyeliner. All the girls wore make-up to school and I didn't want to feel left out.

"It's true that in Islam you're allowed to wear some black eyeliner, but you're putting on way too much," Baba complained. "It's *haram* to make yourself look attractive on purpose when you go out in public."

"All the *khaleeji* girls wear make-up to school, Baba, I'm not the only one," I said as politely as I could. I didn't want to rub him up the wrong way just before school.

"I don't care what the Gulf girls do. If they leapt into a fire would you join them? You shouldn't be so easily influenced by others," he replied sternly.

Perfume wasn't within the means of my teenage budget, but I would buy scented body sprays and spritz those over my *shayla* before I went out. The Gulf girls had the real deal—the latest fragrances by Chanel and Dior.

"You do know that Allah and the Prophet Muhammed, peace be upon him, cursed the woman who wears perfume outside, don't you?" Baba said one morning, as I sat in the back seat of the car on the way to school. "The woman who wears perfume outside is like an adulteress."

"It's just body spray," I mumbled.

"Don't answer me back!" he snapped, and we remained silent for the remainder of the journey to school, the melodic vocals of the man reading the Qur'an on the radio filling the hostile silence.

My brother Ahmed and I had made a new agreement to stay out of each other's business. I found out he'd made friends with a group of boys who were constantly up to no good like smoking weed behind the sheds at break times. I used this new-found information to blackmail him into keeping his mouth shut.

Just like me, Ahmed was struggling to settle into this new culture. I felt like Mum and Baba didn't pay him as much attention as they did our little brother Abdullah.

Abdullah was subservient. We'd moved to the Gulf when he was a young child and he had no idea of the freedoms of the West. All he knew was the blind submission to our parents that was taught to him by his Islamic Studies teachers at Primary School. Unless your parents ask you to leave your religion, you are taught as a Muslim that you must obey them, no matter what. People in the Gulf took this very seriously. A child's opinion or feelings about a matter were never taken into account. Your parents always knew what was best for you.

Ahmed, like Saffa and I, remembered what life was like in England. He remembered what it was like to go to a school where teachers actually cared about their jobs, children had some freedom, and were asked for their viewpoints by adults. In England there were all sorts of extra-curricular activities and clubs you could join outside of school time. I joined the drama club, while Ahmed joined the football club. A child's life in England felt full of promise.

In the Gulf, it was just go to school and then home. The teachers at my new school were mainly from India and Kenya. They weren't on good salaries and had zero enthusiasm. No wonder I counted the hours until school was over.

Ahmed had just turned thirteen and it seemed almost overnight that he lost all his puppy fat. The chubby cheeks Mum had once loved kissing became a distant memory and his voice transformed from that of a chirpy boy to a gruff young man. He insisted on having his hair fully shaved. He hated his brown, curly Egyptian locks and instead he modelled his look on his hero, Vinnie Jones.

He remained relatively polite and well behaved at home, but acted up at school. Almost every week Baba would get a phone call from the deputy head teacher asking him to come in because Ahmed and his friends had made a teacher cry. Ahmed and his friends were known for being disruptive in class and making fun of the teacher's Indian accent. Once Ahmed had shoved a teacher out of his way just because they'd caught him bunking lessons.

"He's on his last chance now," the deputy head teacher told Baba. "One more act of misbehaviour and we'll expel him."

All Baba did was gave him a lecture. It wasn't fair! Every wrong step I took was met with severe measures. But it was only so long before Ahmed pushed Baba too far.

On a relatively calm Saturday afternoon, Baba received a call from the local police station. He jumped up from the sofa and shuffled his shoes on.

"Who was it? What's wrong?" Mum asked when she saw the panic on Baba's face.

"It's Ahmed, he's been arrested," Baba said before he stormed out of the flat, slamming the front door behind him.

"Oh God," Mum said, her eyes raised as if she were pleading to the heavens. "There's never an end to trouble with you children."

It was late in the evening before we heard the key turn in the lock and Baba strode in with Ahmed walking behind him, his head hanging low.

"Caught for stealing chocolates from the local supermarket. The supermarket manager called the police," Baba told Mum.

He held Ahmed up by his t-shirt and marched him into his bedroom, shutting the door behind them. I winced, knowing what was coming next.

The first two whips of Baba's leather belt were met by what

sounded like something in between a yelp and a laugh from Ahmed.

"Are you finding this funny?" Baba shouted, followed by more audible strikes of the belt. "You steal and you ruin my reputation and all you can do is laugh about it?"

"I wasn't laughing!" Ahmed replied.

We heard a thud and Mum, now worried, walked over and opened the bedroom door. Saffa and I tiptoed behind her, staying back far enough to not get noticed. Ahmed was lying on the floor and his face was scarlet.

"Move," Baba said to Mum, and pushed her out of the doorway. "This is all your fault. You treat your children like they're your friends and they have no respect for their father!"

He stormed off to his bedroom and locked the door loudly behind him. As soon as Baba was out of sight, we crowded around Ahmed.

"Do you want to tell me what happened?" Mum asked, helping him to his feet and placing him gently on his bed.

Ahmed held the side of his face. "It wasn't me who stole the chocolates. It was my friend Omar. I was with him and the police arrested me too. I tried to tell them and Baba but no one wanted to hear me out. "

"Wasn't there any CCTV?" Saffa asked.

"Yeah, and it clearly shows Omar stuffing the chocolate bars into his pockets and up his hoodie, but apparently in this country, being with a friend who is committing a crime makes me an accomplice and guilty too. The police gave me a warning."

"But it was just a few chocolate bars, not an armed robbery," I said.

Mum tutted. "That's not the point, Sara. It's chocolate today and then cars tomorrow!"

Ahmed was grounded for two weeks and Baba made him promise he would stop being friends with Omar.

*

It had been two months since my last email to Faisal and my mind was made up. My heart was racing as I sat in my IT lesson and instead of doing my work I opened my email inbox. I clicked 'Sign In' and saw 50 unread emails from him, one for almost every day since I left Egypt. I was scared that if I opened them my dissolve would crumble. I opened a new email to write back to him.

Dear Faisal,
I know you have been waiting for weeks to hear from me. I'm sorry. My dad found out about us while we were on holiday in Egypt and was going to leave me behind to live with my aunt. The only way I was able to come back was to promise to end things with you. So, as much as it kills me, we can't be together anymore. I hope you understand. I will never forget you or the special time we spent together. Promise me you will be brave and grab the first opportunity you get to be free and live independently of your dad.
Sara

I read through my email several times. It was still not too late to discard it. But then I shook my head, closed my eyes, took a deep breath and clicked send. Once I made sure it had been sent successfully, I deactivated my email account.

"So what's the story behind you and your signature red lipstick?" Sophie asked.

Today we were strolling along the South Bank by the River Thames. Springtime had finally arrived and she was wearing a t-shirt while I was wearing a flowy long-sleeved kaftan. It felt like summer even though it was early April.

"For some reason red lipstick was one of those trivial things that really tipped my dad over. It was a little act of rebellion I was brave enough to carry out," I said. "It started when I was at university."

Red Lipstick

When the time had come for me to apply for university, only two options were available: study in Egypt and live with Aunt Mona, or go to the state university in the Gulf. I'd have loved to go to university in England, but Baba said he didn't have the money to send me there, and taking out a student loan was *haram* because you had to pay it back with interest. In Islam, interest is a major sin.

"I'm not going to the state university!" I protested.

Apart from being gender segregated, the state university was well-known for being ruled by a Wahabbi administration. The women's campus had a reputation for being a place where there were predatory lesbian students who assaulted other female students.

"Then don't go to university." Baba shrugged. "Stay at home."

The state university it was.

I got into the state university relatively easily with my good grades. There wasn't much on offer for me in terms of undergraduate programmes. Many of the degrees were taught in Arabic. Although my conversational Arabic was starting to pick up, studying an entire degree in Arabic was unthinkable. So it came down to two choices: English or Political Science.

I'd always been good at English, but in the Gulf the only thing you could do with an English degree was teaching, which wasn't what I wanted. I knew nothing about politics and it was the last subject I would have thought about getting a degree in. Baba's job revolved around politics and it all sounded very boring. In the end, I went for Political Science and got accepted on to the programme. I was the first British student on their programme.

Baba's promotions had afforded us a bigger accommodation. We swapped our flat for a small villa in a respectable part of the city where the rich folk lived. Baba was living the dream. There were enough bedrooms for every one of us kids. No more sharing!

Things improved slightly for Mum too. Baba was adamant that she didn't need to work, that his salary was more than enough for her to be a comfortable housewife. However, he did pay for her to get driving lessons and she passed her test on the first go.

He bought her a little Honda and although she was terrified of highways and only drove to the same handful of places like Abdullah's school, the supermarket and the nearest shopping mall, she didn't feel so trapped at home and her spirits were slightly lifted. She still had to rely on Baba to give her money, but at least she didn't have to depend on him to take her places.

*

The first time Baba officially slut-shamed me was when I got caught going out in public with red lipstick. For three years he'd let me get away with wearing eyeliner and mascara in public, even though he didn't half grumble about it.

I wanted to be like the other women at university, with their glossy hair, immaculate make-up and their *shaylas* perched so perfectly halfway across their heads. I was sick of looking so plain and dowdy.

I bought my first lipstick in secret. My allowance had increased over the years, as Baba's salary increased with promotions. I now received £50 a month in pocket money. It wasn't a massive amount of money, but if I was careful I could buy myself something small and nice once in a while, like a new item of make-up.

I was standing by the Rimmel counter in the local super-market and I hovered over the lipsticks.

"Do you need any help?" the supermarket assistant asked.

"Just browsing," I said.

I was drawn to a shade of bright red. It was brave, it was bold and it was daring—everything I was fighting hard to be. I took it over to the counter and bought it before I could change my mind.

There was nothing that invoked more fury in my father than when he saw my lips painted a scarlet red. I only ever wore the lipstick at home but he still didn't like it.

"In Egypt only the prostitutes wear red lipstick. Take it off," he said when he saw it.

"Come on Baba, I'm at home. You said that it's only *haram* to wear make-up outside."

"Even in front of your father and brothers you should maintain a level of modesty. *Yalla*. Come on, do as I say."

I made sure I huffed loudly before I stormed off to the bathroom and washed the lipstick off. This was getting ridiculous. What would be next?

I complained to Mum once Baba was out of earshot. I could only say so much to Baba before he would lose his temper so just as Mum vented her frustrations to me, I started venting mine to her.

"Baba's rules are insane, Mum," I said as she hung the laundry outside. It was so hot in the Gulf that it only took an hour for laundry to dry. "He'd never have become like this if we'd stayed in London."

"Is this about the red lipstick?" Mum asked as she pegged a pair of Baba's trousers to the washing line.

"Yes! I don't see what the issue is with wearing make-up at home. What does he mean about being modest in front of him, Ahmed and Abdullah? He's my father and they're my little brothers for God's sake. I just don't get it. I don't get *him*."

"I've never got him, Sara."

"Then why are you still with him?"

"What's the alternative? Going to England, taking my *hijab* off so Gran will take me in, and leaving you all behind with him? You can't live here in the Gulf as a foreign woman and a divorcee. My sponsorship would be taken away from me. And I can't get a job here without a university degree."

She was right. In the Gulf there were two types of jobs: respectable jobs and jobs that Arabs looked down at and refused to do. Respectable jobs required a degree. The second category of jobs were supermarket assistants, salespeople, plumbers and cleaners. Jobs that are perfectly respectable in England but here the *khaleeejis* and other Arabs thought they were too good for them. They employed South Asian immigrants to perform these jobs.

Mum wouldn't have been able to be a supermarket assistant, and even if a miracle happened and she was employed as one, the salary wouldn't have been enough to put a roof over her head. There was no such thing as benefits in the Gulf.

*

To an Arab father as conservative as Baba, red lipstick is a flag that marks a woman as a slut who doesn't care about herself or her family's honour. And the most precious thing an Arab woman owns, in the eyes of her father, is her honour.

Eyebrows may be raised if you dare to go out with your lips tinted in a subtle pink lip gloss, but if you dare to brave anything that looks remotely red, you effectively mark yourself as a *sharmootah*, the Arabic word for slut.

Arab parents just don't get that the more you forbid something, the more attractive it becomes. I decided I'd have to be clever and find another way to wear my lipstick.

I'd walk out of the door every morning to go to university au naturel. But once I sat down in my favourite spot at the back of the university bus, I had my red lipstick and compact mirror out. Needless to say, putting on red lipstick while a bus stops and starts and jerks about is not the easiest of tasks!

When I was returning home in the evening after a long day of lectures, I made sure to rub off the lipstick with a make-up wipe before I got off the bus, but the day came when I ran out of make-up wipes. I searched frantically in my handbag for a napkin or a tissue, a piece of paper, even a sanitary towel! I had nothing. I asked the girl sat on the seat beside me if she had a tissue but she shook her head.

If I didn't get this lipstick off by the time the bus rolled up outside my front door, I'd be in trouble. Baba always got home from work before me and he'd be sat in the living room.

I made a *du'aa*, a personal prayer, in my head, praying Allah wouldn't let him be home yet. Seems I was a bit late with my *du'aa* because as the bus turned around that last corner, I saw his black four-wheel drive parked in the driveway. If he saw me, I was done for.

I got off the bus and darted through the front door, aiming straight for the stairs leading to my bedroom, in an attempt to evade Baba's field of vision.

I tried to edge past the corridor sideways, with my back towards the living room where Baba was sat on the sofa, watching the news on the Al Jazeera channel, but he caught a glimpse of me as I went past the doorway.

"Sara," he said. "What's that on your face? Are you wearing red lipstick?"

I froze. I hoped if I didn't answer he'd think I hadn't heard him and he'd let it go. I was so close to the staircase. I took a step.

"Sara! Come here!" he barked.

I sighed and walked slowly to the living room. He lowered the volume of the TV, so the two angry-looking men on the screen were having a silent debate.

"Did I not tell you not to wear red lipstick?" he asked, pointing his wooden prayer beads called *tasbeeh* at me. "Do you enjoy looking like a *sharmootah*?"

I remained silent. Anything I said or did at this point would piss him off even more.

"I asked you a question!" he shouted, the inner ends of his eyebrows pointing downwards. He looked like Bert from *Sesame Street*.

"But Baba, I go to an all-female university—"

He threw a tissue box in my face. On my nose actually, and it hurt more than you'd imagine. I ran up the stairs and slammed my bedroom door before bursting into tears. I buried my head in my pillow, smearing red lipstick and mascara-laden tears into the grey linen. I reached over and grabbed my MP3 player from my bedside table and did what I always did when I got shouted at by Baba: curled up in a foetal position and shared my unspoken angst with Linkin Park.

As soon as I graduated, I'd find a job that would pay enough money to support myself and then I'd move out. And when I moved out, I was going to buy every single shade of red lipstick.

A good Arab woman doesn't leave her father's house unless it's to get married. Any woman who did would be the talk of the community and not someone any decent bachelor would want to marry. But I'd stopped caring.

I was now in my final year at university and it'd be a matter of months before I could get myself a job and finally be free! I couldn't care less if moving out would tarnish Baba's precious reputation. He made us feel like his reputation was more important to him than his children.

Just as I was about to replay Linkin Park's *Crawling* for the third time, Mum quietly opened my bedroom door, and sat down at the end of my bed, the mattress sinking beneath her weight. She had put on 30 kilograms in the five years since moving to the Gulf, as she fought her depression by comfort eating.

"I don't know why you deliberately do things to provoke him," she said, fidgeting with the gold, oval locket she wore around her neck, the one her late grandmother had given to her as a young woman. "It's like you enjoy being told off."

I sat up and stared at her. "I don't see what's wrong with me wearing make-up when I go to an all-female university, riding on an all-female bus!"

"Don't you be rude to me," Mum snapped. But then her voice returned to its normal softness. "I told you before to pick your battles, and red lipstick isn't one of them. How's your nose? Did he break it? I hope he hasn't made more kinks in your nose, it's big enough already."

She tweaked it playfully and I swatted her hand away.

"It's Baba's fault I have a big nose. It's his Arab DNA."

Mum laughed and stood up. "Stop moping about in your bedroom and come downstairs to help me. The *amus* are coming here for a *halaqa* tonight."

"Not again!" I groaned. "We'll be stuck in our bedrooms all night!"

Baba had gone to the mosque to pray *ishaa*, and Mum asked me to help prepare the tea, juices and refreshments. I didn't want to do anything to help Baba. I was still hurt and upset about the tissue box incident.

"Is it alright if I leave you to it?" Mum asked. "I'm exhausted and just want to go to bed."

"Great," I muttered to myself.

"What was that?" Mum asked as she stood in the kitchen doorway.

"Yeah, alright then, I'll do it all," I said loudly.

As soon as Mum went upstairs I thought about a way I could get Baba back for what he had done earlier. I thought about spitting into the cups of tea but then I thought that wasn't good enough, as they wouldn't be able to taste my spit; it would be dissolved in the tea. So I put salt and vinegar into each teacup instead, keeping an ear out for the front door lock. Satisfied, I arranged the tea cups on a tray and put some fruit in a bowl, not bothering to wash it, and took out the Arabic sweets Baba had bought earlier. I put them on our fancy set of silver serving trays which we reserved for Baba's guests.

As soon as I heard Baba's key turning in the lock, I shot upstairs, feeling a rush of adrenaline.

Three hours later, the *amus* had left, and Baba called me down to clear away the trays from the living room. I smirked when I saw that no one had drunk much of their tea. Baba didn't say anything to me about it. The *amus* were too polite as well as fearful of offending their teacher, their *ustaadh*, to say anything about the disgusting tea.

Geology Guy

In the West, most girls are teenagers when they make out with a guy for the first time. When it comes to Arab girls, it's a different ball game. Some wait until they're married to have a physical relationship, or if they're a bit rebellious, they'll kiss during their engagement period.

For a young woman who isn't an Arab, the age of 20 is a bit late to kiss a guy properly for the first time. The pecks that Faisal and I used to give each other when we were in high school were nothing.

After Baba threw the tissue box at my face, I decided not to wear red lipstick outside anymore. I knew I wouldn't be able to get him to compromise on it. I did manage to wear other make-up though: liquid eyeliner, mascara, foundation, concealer and blusher. Baba would frown disapprovingly as I hurried out the front door each morning to catch the university bus.

"You look like Nefertiti," Baba said to me once.

It was a huge step up from being called a slut in Arabic. But he didn't ask me to wash it off. Maybe it was his way of saying this was a compromise. I could wear make-up, just not the red lipstick.

"Nefertiti was a queen," I told him, smiling.

"Your problem is you think you're clever," he said, and he shook his head sorrowfully.

*

During my final year I attended the annual open day at university, which was split into a men's campus and a women's campus. The two campuses were separated by a row of small buildings and corridors, one of which housed the School of Political Science.

The men never crossed over into the women's campus, but the women were allowed on to the men's campus for events like the open day. It was a rare opportunity to mix with the male students. Most of the female students—who had limited interactions with males—made the most of this event by wearing their tightest *abayas*, highest heels and so much make-up you'd think they were auditioning for *RuPaul's Drag Race*.

I wasn't particularly interested in going to the open day again but my closest friend at the university, Heba, was running the stall for our Political Science programme, so I decided to pay her a visit.

Heba was Egyptian and had lived most of her life in the Gulf. Her parents were secular Muslim Egyptians who were cool with Heba dating, going to parties and even drinking. Heba didn't wear the *hijab* and her staple university outfit was a polo T-shirt with tight jeans that hugged her hourglass figure.

She had a mane of enviable brown curls and was naturally beautiful. She didn't have to wear a slick of make-up. She was sassy, not afraid to speak her mind and the Gulf girls held her in high regard.

Muneera, my friend from high school, had joined the same university a year after me, but we'd drifted apart. We seemed to view the Gulf women very differently. Muneera hung out with a group I called the Barbies. They were superficial young women who came to uni in their most expensive, glamorous clothes. They sat at Starbucks, sipping their frappes, gossiping instead of attending their lectures.

The Barbies were the girls who would take off their headscarves and *niqabs* as soon as their drivers dropped them at the main gates of the university. They'd flood the bathrooms and hog the mirrors to paint their faces in bright shades of makeup and backcomb their hair to within an inch of its life. Yeah, not my type of girls.

Soon after starting university I decided to start wearing an *abaya* with my *shayla*. Not because I'd suddenly become religious, but because I was so sick of Baba telling me off if my tops didn't cover my bum or if I was wearing something, which to me was loose, but he thought was tight.

I asked him to buy me a couple of *abayas* to wear over my clothes for uni and he happily agreed. Covering myself up more must have been music to his ears.

As I stood with Heba at her stall, we noticed the guy at the stall across from us looking our way. He was tall, broad-shouldered, dark and handsome. He was wearing a white *thowb*, and a red and white chequered headdress—the *shemaagh*—arranged on his head in a style they called the half-cobra. It had one piece of fabric carefully folded over his round black *egaal* and the other piece fell elegantly behind his head.

"He's checking you out," Heba whispered in my ear.

"Don't be silly," I said, rolling my eyes. "You're the pretty one. He's looking at you. Hot guys like him don't look at me."

"He really isn't. Besides, you look like a Gulf girl with your *abaya* and *shayla*. They aren't interested in girls who aren't covered like me. I'm going to turn around and you see if he keeps looking." Heba turned around.

Lo and behold, she was right! The hot guy was looking directly at me and smiling.

"Damn, he is looking at me!" I told her between clenched teeth.

"You have to go over there and get his number," Heba said, giving me a gentle push.

"No way!" I said, shaking her hand off me. "Are you forgetting something? I don't have a mobile phone!"

Yes, that's right. I was twenty and still not allowed a phone.

"Oh, sorry, I forgot. I tell you what, you can have my second mobile phone. It's my old Nokia. If he asks for your number, just give him the number of that phone."

"I don't know, Heba. . ."

"Come on Sara! You need to live a little and what you need is a boyfriend!"

I knew Heba was only trying to help but if I got caught with a mobile phone at home, Baba would confiscate it and then what? I wouldn't have any money to buy her a replacement phone.

"I'll think about the phone," I said.

Heba rolled her eyes. "And the guy? At least go and say hi."

I glanced over at him and he was showing a flyer to someone. Saying hello wouldn't hurt.

"Okay, cool."

"That's my girl," Heba said, winking at me.

I walked casually past the other stalls first, pretending to be interested in them, so it wouldn't be so obvious that I was coming to his stall just to talk to him.

"Welcome to the Geology Programme." He smiled and I was taken aback. His whole face lit up when he smiled, exposing his perfect, symmetrical, white teeth. "Are you interested in joining our undergraduate programme next year?"

"Not really, I'm already in my final year," I said. "I'm having a look at options for my brother. He's about to finish high school."

It wasn't a total lie. Ahmed was about to finish high school. I just hadn't planned on helping him apply for university.

"Great! We have a whole information pack I can give to you for him." He took out a big folder, which I tried not to groan at. I'd have to carry that around with me for the rest of the day. "I'm graduating at the end of this year too." He handed over the folder.

When he looked at me with those big brown eyes under those long black eyelashes, my stomach did a somersault.

Geology Guy went on to show me photos of his department and an exploding model volcano he'd made for the open day. I tried my best to look interested when really I was just interested in him.

"Would it be okay to swap email addresses?" he asked. "It'd be good to keep in touch and I can help your brother if he chooses to apply for our programme?"

Talking online would buy me some time while making a decision on taking Heba's phone. I took out a pen and spiral pad from my bag, ripped out a piece of paper and jotted down my email address. He took out his fancy silver ballpoint from the chest pocket of his perfectly ironed *thowb* and wrote his email address on my writing pad.

When he handed it to me, I noticed the time on his Rolex watch.

"I need to get going. I have a lecture soon, but it was really cool meeting you."

"No worries," he said. "Don't forget to add me on Windows Live Messenger."

"I'll add you this evening!" I replied, waving at him as I left.

Aziz

I couldn't wait to finish my lectures.

As soon as I got home, I ran up the staircase to our upstairs lounge where we had our family computer, threw my rucksack down, and logged on to Windows Live Messenger. I added Geology Guy to my contact list and he appeared straight away. His name was Aziz.

I felt a rush of excitement. What should I say? Would I seem desperate starting the conversation first? I took a deep breath. *Play it cool, Sara.*

I opened the BBC News website, barely reading the articles. A minute later, I got a notification telling me that Aziz was saying hello!

I typed back quickly in Arabic.

ME: *Hi Aziz!*

AZIZ: *Is this the pretty lady I met at the open day earlier?*

Oh my God, he thinks I'm pretty!

ME: *Yes, it is the pretty lady from the open day. Is this the handsome man who was running the geology stall?*

AZIZ: *Lol I don't think I'm handsome, but yes, I was running the geology stall.*

ME: *Well if you don't think you're handsome, I suggest you go get your eyes checked at the optician's*

My flirting skills weren't the smoothest. Neither were his. Flirting wasn't something I was used to doing.

AZIZ: *Beautiful and a sense of humour. A lady like you must be engaged or married already?*

ME: *No, I'm single.*

AZIZ: *I don't get how you're a convert to Islam yet you speak Arabic so well.*

ME: *Oh I'm not a convert lol. My mother is English and my father is Arab. I was raised Muslim.*

AZIZ: *Mashallah. Are you free to go out for a coffee after you're done with your lectures tomorrow?*

Wow, he definitely didn't waste time. I thought about my schedule for the next day. There were only two university buses running in the afternoon—one at two o'clock and one at five. I finished at three which meant I had two hours to leave campus, have coffee with him and be back on campus before the wheels of the bus started rolling. Scheduling a coffee in the evening wouldn't work. I'd have to come up with an elaborate story for Baba about why I needed to go out and that's if he even bought it.

ME: *I finish at 3 o'clock tomorrow, but I don't drive so I need to be back on campus for 5 o'clock so I don't miss the second bus.*

AZIZ: *I can give you a ride home, no problem.*

ME: *Thank you but my father will be home from work by then and he'll be able to see me getting out of your car from the window.*

AZIZ: *I can drop you off around the corner?*

ME: *That still won't work. We have neighbours who are my dad's friends and if they see they'll tell him. Plus, he waits to hear the sound of the bus dropping me off—sorry!*

AZIZ: *OK, how about I pick you up from the main car park in the men's campus and I'll drop you back to the campus before 5?*

ME: *Deal.*

ME: *Great! What's your phone number?*

A wave of panic surged over me. Of course he'd ask for a phone number! How else would we communicate away from a computer? It looked like I'd have to take up Heba's offer after all. I gave him Heba's second mobile number.

AZIZ: *See you tomorrow at 3.*

ME: *See you then!*

I couldn't believe it. I was going on a date with Aziz. I grabbed the cordless phone and took it to my room, closed the door and called Heba to tell her the exciting news. She sounded even more excited than I was.

"I'm telling you, he's going to be your boyfriend!" she squealed.

"It's just a coffee, Heba. He's not going to be my boyfriend! We're just going out as friends."

"Bullshit! He thinks you're cute, you think he's hot, and you two are going to end up getting together."

I laughed. "I'm glad you have higher expectations than I do. I gave him your number for the other phone like you suggested. Can you bring your phone to university tomorrow please? And if he sends a text message, don't read it!"

"Err, it's still my phone until 9:45am tomorrow," she said. "I'm joking! Trust me, if he texts tonight I won't read the messages."

"You're the best. Oh, I was wondering, you've had guys pick you up from university loads of times, do security ever stop cars at the main gate and ask for ID? You know, to check if the girl and the guy are related? I heard they do."

Heba laughed. "Girl, that was before our time at the university. No one checks anymore. Don't be worried."

I found it difficult to sleep that night. I was excited, but nervous. What if the security guard decided to stop the car and ask us for our national ID cards? Then he'd figure out we weren't related and we'd be pulled aside. He'd call the police who would then call my father, and he'd take me home, beat me, and ground me for life. I'd have to say goodbye to being a graduate and my future plans of being an independent woman with my own place.

I wondered whether I should get up, creep into the lounge to the family computer and send Aziz an email saying that I couldn't do it. After everything that had happened in high school with Faisal, was I going to put myself at risk of getting caught and being in serious trouble again?

Everyone was out there meeting guys, falling in love and having a life… except me. I had to be more careful this time. I have to live a little or my life would be as boring and closed as the *salafi amus'* daughters who weren't even allowed to watch TV. Okay, that was a bit of an extreme comparison.

Heba had gone out with guys and left from the men's campus plenty of times. But it was because she was uncovered. Everyone keeps an eye on the covered girls, waiting for them to step one toe out of line before coming down on them with full force. According to the Wahabbis that ran the university, uncovered women were already fallen women, so in their view they were hopeless cases who didn't need saving.

I had made up my mind. I was going live my life on the dangerous side.

The Date

It was hard to focus on my lectures the next day. Heba gave me the mobile phone in the morning, and I saw there was one unread text message. I opened it and it was Aziz asking me to me meet him at the men's car park at three.

Make sure you cover your face with your shayla, he said at the end of the text message.

"Erm, controlling much?" I showed Heba the message.

"It's what all the Gulf girls do when they go out on a date. Do you want to risk one of the professors who knows your dad seeing you and telling him they saw you leaving the university in a car with a guy?" she asked.

No I didn't. I texted him back that I'd see him at three.

I spent my lectures fantasising about my date. I wondered where he was going to take me. I willed time to move faster but five minutes felt like an hour. Maybe we'll go to a café and have coffee in a cosy corner? I'll make him laugh and he'll be hypnotised by me.

Three o'clock finally rolled around and having purposely chosen a seat near the lecture room door, I bolted out the second my professor wrapped up the lecture. I took out my newly acquired phone and sent Aziz a text to say I was walking to the agreed meeting point.

Once I'd passed through one of the corridors that separated the women's campus from the men's campus, I took the end of my black *shayla* and put it sideways over my face, making a makeshift face veil that Gulfies called a *ghishwa*. The *shayla* was made out of chiffon, so it was translucent enough for me to see where I was going and not bump into something.

I got a text back saying he was already there waiting for me. My heart was beating so hard and fast that I could feel it through my back. I tried not to walk too fast. I didn't want to attract any unnecessary attention.

Once I'd approached the car park, I saw a white Land Cruiser waiting with Aziz inside. I walked up to the passenger side of the car, opened the door and hoisted myself up on to the seat.

"You made it," he said, smiling at me.

He was so good-looking it made my ovaries hurt!

"I did." *Smooth, Sara.*

"Let's get out of the campus and decide where we want to go once we're on the road. Don't worry, we'll be back in time so you don't miss the bus."

We drove towards the main gates and as we got closer, my hands started to sweat, but the security guard didn't even glance our way. He lifted the barrier without a second look, and we drove straight out. I couldn't believe how easy it was.

"I have an idea," Aziz said, as we drove down the main road. "How about we pick up *karak* from a roadside café and drink it in the car by the sea? The coast is nearby."

Karak was a sugary tea made with lots of milk, cardamom, cloves and cinnamon that had been imported with Indian immigrants and had become a favourite of the locals.

Sipping *karak* by the sea? It all sounded so romantic.

My eyes lit up. "I guess we can go to the coast for an hour."

He grinned. "Great!"

We picked up two cups of *karak* from a little tea room and I was impressed by how polite Aziz was to the waiter who came outside and served him at the car window. He even gave him a tip. I'd seen other Gulf guys bark orders at Indian waiters, but Aziz was well-mannered and softly spoken. It made me like him even more.

The local coastline was only a short drive. He parked the car on a quiet spot in the sand that looked directly upon the brilliant turquoise seawater. It seemed to glitter under the bright sun.

"Wow," I said, taken aback by its beauty.

"Now are you happy we came?" he asked, and I nodded.

A love song by Mohammed Abdu, the Saudi Arabian superstar, played low on the car radio. I removed my *shayla* from my face.

"You're so beautiful," Aziz said, and he took my hand in his.

My hand looked tiny compared to his. I felt dizzy with excitement. I then made the classic mistake of drinking my *karak* without allowing it to cool first.

"What's wrong?" he asked as I grimaced in pain.

"I've burned my mouth."

"I know something that will help take away the pain," he replied, looking sheepish.

He took both of our cups and placed them in the car's cup

holders and before I knew it, he'd leaned over and kissed me forcefully on my lips.

I was super naïve when it came to being physical with a guy. I didn't know how to react. I froze with my lips firmly pressed together as he tried to pry them open with his. He loosened my *shayla* with his fingers so he could kiss my neck. It wasn't a gentle, soft kiss like the type you see in Hollywood movies. It felt like a vacuum cleaner had been applied to my neck. I could feel his lips and tongue sucking at my flesh and it started to hurt. Then he rubbed my thighs roughly with his hands.

If he thought he was turning me on, he was way off! I felt like I was being manhandled.

I really wanted to say, *Stop, that's enough*, but I didn't. The words felt stuck in my throat.

I'd always dreamt that my first kiss with a man would be as magical as Ryan Gosling and Rachel McAdams's famous scene in *The Notebook*, not a scene from *Dumb and Dumber*.

"What's wrong? Why aren't you kissing me back?" he asked, finally stopping to take a breath.

"I'm scared someone will see us," I lied as I gently pushed him off me.

"There's no one here," he said, leaning in towards me for some more vacuum cleaner action.

I turned my head quickly to the side and looked over at the clock above the car radio and saw that it was 4:40pm already. I'd been saved by the clock.

"We need to be getting back, or I'll miss my bus," I said.

He glanced over at the clock, looking disappointed. "I guess you're right."

I pulled down the sun shield and took a look at my neck in the mirror. There were love bites all over it.

"How am I going to go home like this?" I exclaimed.

"Do you have liquid foundation? Cover them with that, it'll work," he said matter-of-factly, as if he was an expert on covering up love bites. Maybe he was?

"If my father sees them he'll kill me."

"He won't," Aziz said, sounding bored. "Men don't pay attention to these things."

"My father is a man who does."

"Let's get you to the bus on time," he said and he started the car.

All those butterflies I'd felt earlier had taken flight and disappeared into the sky. As he drove us back, I peered over to look at him through the black material of my *shayla* which was now covering my face. What a douchebag.

I arrived back at the university with just ten minutes to spare.

"I'll text you this evening," Aziz said.

"Okay, see you." I hurried out of the car, and power-walked back to the women's campus to the university bus stop.

I honestly didn't want to hear back from him. Hiding these love bites from Baba was the only thing I cared about.

Once I got home, I headed straight for the ground-floor bathroom with my bag. I locked the door, took off my *shayla* and looked at my neck in the mirror. There were now dark red bruises all over my neck.

I took my liquid foundation out of my make-up bag and lathered it all over my neck using my fingers. I tried to blend it in as best as I could so the colour of my neck didn't look distinctly different to my face. I could still see a little redness poking through the foundation, but it would have to do.

I went upstairs to my room and instead of wearing a *jalabiyya*, an ankle-length Arabic nightdress, I changed into a turtle-neck top and a maxi skirt, then came downstairs to help Mum set the table for dinner.

"Why are you wearing a turtle neck? It's been boiling hot today!" Mum asked as soon as I walked into the kitchen.

"I'm feeling a bit chilly," I said, taking out cutlery from the kitchen drawers.

"Are you coming down with something?" she asked, spooning white rice into a serving dish.

"Er. . . I'm not sure," I replied, and went next door to put out the cutlery and placemats on the dining table.

The entire family sat down and we ate our stewed lamb and peas with rice. No one seemed to notice anything. As usual, the majority of the dinner passed in silence, as no one could think of a topic of conversation Baba would engage in. There was never any silence at the dinner table on the days where he was out in the evening. The house would be filled with laughter and jokes.

After dinner, I went upstairs and changed into my long *jalabiyya* and wrapped a *shayla* around my neck. I decided to spend the rest of the evening studying in my bedroom, but Mum called me downstairs to the kitchen.

"Can you hang the laundry outside?" She handed me the bucket.

As I bent down to take the wet clothes out of the washing machine, the *shayla* slipped and fell on the floor.

"Why does your neck look weird and blotchy? Is that liquid foundation on your neck?" she asked, walking towards me.

I felt like I was going to be sick. "I've got some sort of weird rash on my neck and it looks ugly. I was just trying to cover it up," I said quickly.

"Oh, okay, rub off the make-up and let me have a look," she said.

Shit.

I rubbed off just a bit and she came and took a closer look.

"That looks like an allergic reaction," she said. "I'm going to give you an antihistamine tablet but if it's not better in the morning we're going to the GP."

"Okay, thanks," I said, turning my back on her to take the clothes out. Mum wandered into the living room.

As I lifted up the bucket full of wet clothes, I froze. What if the doctor realises I have love bites?

I spent most of the night unable to sleep, tossing and turning. There was no way the love bites would be gone by the morning. Stupid Aziz. He hadn't even had the decency to check if I was okay.

*

Morning came and Mum took another look at my neck and insisted that she take me to the GP.

The local medical centre was split into two sections, one for men and one for women, with male doctors on the men's side and female doctors on the women's side. We entered through the ladies' entrance and took a ticket. We had to wait for our number to appear on the screen above the reception before I could be registered as a walk-in patient and be seen.

I sat nervously for half an hour, praying that the doctor would just take a quick look and prescribe me something. When it was finally my turn, I went inside the doctor's office, and I thanked God that Mum decided to sit outside in the ladies' waiting room.

"So how can I help you today?" the doctor asked, her hands neatly folded on her desk.

"I have a rash on my neck that appeared yesterday out of nowhere."

"Do you have any other symptoms? A high temperature? A headache? Stomach pain?"

"No, they're just itchy."

"Do you mind if I have a look?"

"No, not at all."

She stood up, snapped some rubber gloves on and walked over to me. She stretched the skin on my neck with her rubbery fingers, then bent over and started whispering so the nurse sitting in the far left corner of the room couldn't hear her.

"Did someone do this to you? Did someone at home hurt you?"

"What do you mean?"

"Is someone abusing you?" the doctor asked. "These look very aggressive."

"Oh no! No one touched me!"

"It's okay, this is a safe place. Whatever you tell me is in confidence and I'll only inform the police if you want me to," she continued.

Inform the police? I didn't need that!

"No, no, I swear by Allah no one at home did this to me."

"Okay, then it must be some sort of reaction to something you touched or ate," she said. "I'll write a prescription for some stronger antihistamines and cream for the itchiness, but I want you to go with the nurse to get an antihistamine injection."

I prayed that taking strong antihistamines when you didn't need them wouldn't cause any internal damage. But it was better than the doctor telling the police I'd been strangled, or her realising they were love bites.

I went off with the nurse to get my injection and not long after that I was allowed to leave.

"I'm so glad it's just an allergic reaction," Mum said as she drove us home. "For a second I thought they were love bites and then I realised you're not that type of girl."

I laughed nervously. "Right, Mum."

I was in the living room and I felt Heba's phone vibrate in my bra—my hiding spot for it. I went to the bathroom and took the phone out. It was a text message from Aziz. I scanned it and had to stop myself from throwing the phone at the wall. Was he kidding me?

I thought women from Britain were open-minded and easy but you're just cold and frigid.

I typed *asshole* but deleted it. I didn't need to stoop to his level.

May Allah forgive you, I typed back.

Then I went to bed and cried myself to sleep.

"So I have to ask," Sophie said. "Did you get any reaction from the antihistamines?"

I laughed. "No, thankfully I was okay. And no-one apart from Aziz knew about the love bites."

"Amazing." Sophie grinned. "Do you need a break or shall we keep going?"

I stretched out my neck. "Let's keep going."

Phone

Saffa was now in Year 11 and doing her GCSEs. She had a Syrian boyfriend in the same year at school called Kareem. Kareem had given her a mobile phone so they could keep in touch outside school. Only I knew about her boyfriend and mobile phone.

Abdullah was in a government school on account of his excellent Arabic skills—Baba invested all his hopes in him being the perfect Arab son—and Ahmed, who was with Saffa at the same co-ed international high school I'd been at, was more of an English lad than an Arab one, which meant he couldn't care less about what Saffa and I got up to.

"I'm really sorry about that time I snitched on you to Baba in Egypt about your ex Faisal," Ahmed told me one day when it was just the two of us at home. We were sat on the living room sofa side by side, playing *Call of Duty*.

"It was a long time ago and you were young," I replied, trying to reassure him.

Ahmed paused the game and turned to look at me. "Baba was alright with me back then. Then the day I got arrested

92

everything changed. Things between me and him have never been the same. It's like I lost his respect forever."

"I feel exactly the same way." I sighed. "Believe me, when Abdullah becomes a teenager and starts rebelling like all normal teenagers, Baba won't adore him so much."

We weren't jealous of Abdullah. We'd all been Baba's favourite at one point during our childhood.

"The truth is, I don't think Baba knows how to handle teenagers," Ahmed continued.

Ahmed had hit the nail on the head. That was exactly it— Baba confused normal teenage behaviour for disrespect and disobedience, which he thought was a personal attack on him.

"That's the deepest thing you've said in ages," I said, laughing, trying to keep things light-hearted. "Now let's finish this game before the rest of the family come home and Abdullah asks me for his handset back."

When we shared a room, I'd hear Saffa whispering on the phone to her boyfriend Kareem in the middle of the night. Now that she had her own room, it was easier for her to talk to him. It had been a wonder to me over the past year how Mum and Baba hadn't walked past her bedroom and heard her, but I was happy that the stars were in her favour.

A few weeks after my forced make-out session (thankfully the love bites had finally faded), I came home to see a shouting match between Saffa and Abdullah in the living room. Mum was standing in between them trying to play referee. Ahmed was out with his friends, no doubt up to no good. Baba wasn't at home either.

In Abdullah's hand was Saffa's mobile phone. "I'm telling Baba. I heard you speaking to a boy! I'm going to stay up and wait until he comes home, even if it's past midnight," Abdullah shouted, waving the phone just out of her reach.

"I was speaking to my friend Maryam and it's her phone! Check the call log!" Saffa shrieked.

"Why do you even have a mobile phone? You know you're not allowed one."

"It's none of your business," Saffa said. "I needed a phone and I knew Baba wasn't going to buy one for me, so Maryam gave me her old one. Now give it back. It doesn't belong to me!"

"But I heard a boy's voice coming from your phone," Abdullah said, narrowing his eyes. "Who were you speaking to? Do you have a boyfriend?"

"It was Maryam," Saffa said, lunging forward.

Abdullah, despite only being twelve was much taller, with gangly arms and legs, and he held the phone high above Saffa's head.

"Stop it! That's enough!" Mum yelled.

Saffa dug her long nails into his arm and he howled and dropped the phone on to the rug. Without a moment's hesitation Saffa snatched the phone off the rug and ran upstairs to her bedroom.

"Abdullah, go to your room. I need to talk to Mum," I said.

I expected him to answer me back, but he was teary-eyed, clutching his arm, which now had blood-infused grooves, and he quietly went upstairs without protest.

Mum sank into the living room sofa and began to cry. "I'm just so sick of the drama every day in this house. I stayed with your father all these years for all of you, so that you wouldn't have a broken family, and you kids repay me by constantly fighting."

94

I sat down and put my arm around her shoulder. "Don't say that, Mum, they're teenagers. It's normal for siblings to fight."

Mum looked up at me. "Do you think Saffa is talking to a boy?"

"I'm sure she wouldn't be daft enough to make the same mistake I did. I'll talk to her about returning her friend's phone before she gets in trouble with Baba. What are we going to do about Abdullah though?"

"I'll talk to him before I go to bed," Mum said, wiping away her tears with a tissue. "God knows if he'll listen to me though."

Before I went to bed, I knocked on Saffa's bedroom door.

"Who is it?" she snapped.

"It's me," I whispered.

"Oh, okay. Come in."

I quietly opened the door to find her sitting in bed in the dark, staring down at the mobile phone, which lay cradled between her hands.

"Saffa, you need to give that phone back to Kareem tomorrow," I said softly.

"I'll hide it."

"You know that's a stupid idea. Baba will search high and low for it."

"I have a place in the back yard that he won't even think of."

"He'll find it, believe me. Save yourself a fight and give it to Kareem."

"Fine, whatever. I'll give it back to him."

"Promise me, Saffa."

"I promise, I promise," she grumbled, and pulled her duvet over her head.

I found it hard to sleep that night. What would happen if Abdullah ignored Mum's pleas not to snitch on Saffa to Baba? Would he send her to Egypt to live with Aunt Mona?

Sisters

The next day was torturous as my lectures and seminars went by at a snail's pace. I just wanted to go home and find out whether Abdullah had kept his mouth shut.

"What do you think, Sara?" my favourite lecturer, Professor Munthir, asked.

I had no clue what he was referring to.

The professor frowned. "Are you feeling unwell? You can leave if you are. I won't mark you as absent."

"It's okay, I'll be fine," I said, sitting up and straightening myself out in my chair.

That evening, I was sitting at the dining table revising my Economics module for a mid-term exam. The minute I saw Baba walk through the door, I knew from his face that Abdullah had told him. He had that expression of pure disgust he wore when one of us had done something he deemed shameful.

"Where's Saffa?" he growled.

"Upstairs," I replied quietly.

"Tell her to come down," he ordered.

I ran upstairs and opened Saffa's bedroom door, where she was inside studying on her bed.

"Saffa, please tell me you gave the phone back today."

"I did, first thing."

"Okay, because Baba's here," I said. "And he wants you to come downstairs. Don't worry, I've got your back."

She started to cry. Every tear felt like a dagger in my heart.

"I don't want to go downstairs!"

I didn't know what to do. I held my hand out to her.

"Come downstairs, I'll stand beside you."

"But you can't protect me if he decides to hit me," she said. She was right.

"Well. . . I'll call the police if he touches you."

"Are you dumb?" Saffa snapped, and I quickly shushed her. "The police here won't do anything if he tells them it's a family matter and that I'm in a relationship with a boy."

She was right again.

"I'm not going down to him," she said, and she stayed put on her bed.

I had no choice but to go back downstairs without her.

"Didn't I ask you to tell Saffa to come downstairs?" he barked. "Where is she?"

"She's studying for her exams," I replied.

Baba's face turned bright red. "I don't care about her bloody exams! I told her to do something, so she has to do it! Move." He pushed past me and made his way upstairs.

I followed him as he stormed over to Saffa's bedroom and burst through the door. He yanked her off the bed with one hand, pulling her by the arm, and slapped her hard across the face.

"Why do you and your sister constantly disobey me? You want to make me look like a fool? How many times did I tell you not to speak to boys and you disobey me?"

He slapped her again and she tried to put her arms up in defence.

"Please Baba," I begged. "Saffa hasn't done anything. Abdullah is lying, she wasn't speaking to a boy. It was her friend Maryam. I checked."

He ignored me and kept hitting her across the face and head. She was crying hysterically, which made me start crying too. I saw movement by the door and looked over to see Mum and Abdullah watching and not saying a word. Mum flinched every time Baba hit Saffa.

"What's going on?" Ahmed appeared in the doorway. His firm stance made him look like a cross between Superman and Vinnie Jones. "Why are you hitting her?"

Ahmed was strong, even stronger than Baba. Baba paused and kept glancing between Ahmed and Saffa as if asking himself whether he could carry on hitting Saffa without Ahmed getting in the way.

Baba let go of Saffa and dramatically clutched the pinstriped fabric of his work shirt.

"You kids are killing me! You're making me ill. I have diabetes and high blood pressure because of you." He glared at Saffa. "Where's the phone? Give me the phone!"

"I gave it back already," Saffa said in between hysterical sobs.

"Enough lying! Give me the phone or I'll forbid you from sitting your exams."

"Baba, she gave the phone back to her friend Maryam," I told him.

"You're both liars. I don't believe either of you," he said, giving me a disgusted look before turning back to Saffa who was holding the side of her face that was turning a fierce shade of red. "You're not leaving your bedroom. There's no school until you give me the phone. I don't care if you miss your exams."

He marched out of the room, slamming the door behind him.

"This is some bullshit," Ahmed said. "I'm going out."

Abdullah hung his head and left the room. Mum, Saffa and I stood in silence yet we spoke a thousand words.

*

I needed to come up with a plan quickly to help Saffa so that she wouldn't miss her GCSEs. Ahmed was all fists, temper and brawn, but not very strategic when it came to dealing with Baba. I needed to come up with something on my own.

The best thing I could think of was roping in her boyfriend Kareem. He had a twin sister called Haya who knew Saffa was his girlfriend. I was certain Haya would help.

I went into Saffa's room as she was lying on her bed, staring at the ceiling. She wasn't crying anymore but her eyes were red and swollen.

"Saffa, give me Kareem's number. I'm going to tell him what happened today with Baba. We can ask Haya to tell Baba that she's Maryam and she gave you the phone to keep in touch for help with school revision."

Saffa sat up. "That could work. Pass me that pen and piece of paper on my bedside table."

I handed them to her and she wrote Kareem's number.

"But how are you going to call Kareem? The landline can't call mobile phones anymore since Baba disabled that service."

I took out Heba's mobile phone from my bra. I often wonder how much radiation I exposed my boobs to over those years.

Saffa gasped. "You have one too? How?"

"Shh," I said, putting it back into my bra quickly. "It's Heba's phone."

I went to the bathroom, took out Heba's phone and sent a text message to Kareem.

Hi Kareem. This is Saffa's sister. Our little brother overheard Saffa speaking to you on her mobile phone and snitched on her to our dad. She won't be at school tomorrow. Our dad doesn't believe she gave the phone back. We told him it belongs to a friend called Maryam and that she was speaking to Maryam on the phone when she got caught. We said the phone was for calling Maryam when she needed help with revision. Please can you ask Haya to help us out and pretend to be Maryam? Can you arrange with Haya that we call on the number you gave to Saffa and that she picks up?

I didn't have to wait long for Kareem to text me back.

This is mad! I wish I could speak to your dad and stand up for Saffa, but I know that's impossible. I spoke to Haya and she said she will help. Call Saffa's number from your dad's phone and Haya will pick up.

With Baba in such a foul mood, it wasn't the best time to go to him and ask him to call Haya to prove Saffa's innocence. We would need to give Baba a day to cool down a little.

Thank you so much Kareem! And please tell Haya thank you from me. I'll call her tomorrow at 7pm.

I tucked my phone back into my bra, flushed the toilet so my family would think I'd just used it and washed my hands for good measure. Everything I did in my life felt so calculated. For everything I planned to do, I needed to think of all the "what-ifs" first.

The next evening at 7pm, after Baba had finished his dinner, I waited till he was sat on the sofa, *tasbeeh* beads in one hand, and a cup of tea in the other.

"Baba, I've had a thought. Why don't we call the number Maryam gave Saffa? If she picks up it'll prove Saffa was really given the phone by a girl and that she gave the phone back like she said she did."

Baba frowned. I held my breath.

"Give me my phone. It's over there charging," he eventually said, gesturing with his fingers towards the TV stand.

I unplugged the phone from the charger, punched in the number and handed it over to Baba once it started to ring. I heard a female voice pick up.

Yes, Haya had come through!

Baba had turned the call volume up so high that I was able to hear her from across the room.

"Hello?" Haya said.

"*Assalamu alaikum*, peace be upon you. This is Saffa's father. Is this her friend Maryam?"

"*Wa alaikum assalam*, and peace be upon you *amu*, yes it is."

"How's your family? Is everyone well? How are your studies going? Are you ready for your exams?"

I had to restrain myself from rolling my eyes at his fake concern.

"Revision is going well. I'm sorry if I caused any issues," Haya said. "I just gave Saffa my second phone temporarily because she needed help with her maths revision during the evenings, and I'm not able to come over to study at your house every day."

"No problem, it's not an issue. Saffa wasn't feeling well today, but she'll be back at school tomorrow, *inshallah*. Give my regards to your parents."

My plan had worked!

Baba ended the call and motioned at me to put his phone back on the charger.

"Tell Saffa she can go back to school from tomorrow. And if she has an issue with her studies she should come and talk to me. I'd have gotten her a maths tutor. She shouldn't go behind my back and disobey me."

"No problem Baba, I'll go and tell her," I replied.

I went to Saffa's room where she was sat on the edge of her bed, waiting nervously.

She perked up when she saw me.

"Did it work?" she asked, her voice full of hope.

"It worked!"

Saffa put her hand over her heart and took a massive sigh of relief. "I really thought I was going to miss my GCSEs! I'm so lucky to have such a good sister. Thank you, Sara."

She stood up and gave me a massive hug. I kissed her on the cheek before resting my chin on the top of her head.

"That's what big sisters are for," I said.

Cinderella

It was coming up to my best friend Heba's birthday and every year she'd have a house party to celebrate. Boys were invited and there was lots of alcohol. The party would run into the early hours. In the three years I'd known her at university I hadn't been to a single one. Every year she invited me and I always declined, and instead I would take her out for dinner with our Gulf girlfriends.

This year it was her 21st birthday, which made it legal for her to have her birthday in one of the few bars or nightclubs, all located within a five-star hotels. There were no standalone bars or nightclubs in this country. Special licences were given to five-star hotels to serve alcohol and the police turned a blind eye.

"It's the big one," Heba told me over lunch one day at university. "And you have to come, Sara! I won't take no for an answer."

"Let's just say we come up with a plan so I can come, are you forgetting that I'm not twenty-one? How will I gain entry to a bar?"

"Oh, that's easily sorted," Heba said, in between mouthfuls of her southern fried chicken wrap. "It's on a Friday, so you tell your dad one of the women at university is getting married and you're going with me. Then I can pick you up Friday afternoon so we can get ready together. You can sleep over at mine. I'll talk to your dad if I have to. And I can easily get hold of another girl's ID card—we can pretend it's yours."

"That's a really risky idea," I said anxiously. "What if the bouncer doesn't think the girl on the ID card looks like me? Where will I go if I can't get into the bar? I can't go home after that."

"Don't you worry, you'll get in. I'm friends with the bar's owner. I've used other girls' ID cards loads of times." She winked at me.

I'd never been to a real party. You know, like the ones you see in movies with boys, alcohol and amazing music. I can't lie, I was seriously tempted to go.

There was another issue with going to Heba's birthday at the bar. You weren't allowed to wear your *hijab* in bars and nightclubs here. I'd have to remove it.

I'd never removed my headscarf in public since the day I put it on at age twelve. In Islam the moment your period starts you're expected to wear the *hijab*.

Baba had never explained the story behind wearing a headscarf and why it was a necessary part of our religion. He just said it was compulsory. Because of that it made no sense to me why my hair was an object of attraction that needed hiding away from the opposite sex. He said—more than once—that if I ever took it off, I wouldn't be his daughter. It was out of fear that I kept my headscarf on.

I was also worried about going into a hotel with Heba and her friends and having one of Baba's friends recognise me. If Baba ever found out, it'd mean a beating and being grounded for life. I needed to think about this and the logistics very carefully, and then ask Baba when he was in one of his rare good moods.

A couple of nights later, Baba was in a very good mood because he'd been promoted again at work. It was the perfect time to ask him to go to the imaginary wedding with Heba.

After we'd eaten the chocolate fudge cake he'd bought in celebration, I worked up the courage to ask him. My heart was beating wildly as it always did when I was asking him for something.

"It's one of the *khaleeji* girls at university's wedding this coming Friday. Can I go? It won't finish until 2am so Heba's offered to pick me up, let me sleep over, and drop me back home on Saturday."

He took a sip of his red tea. "I'll need to speak to one of Heba's parents first."

One of her parents? I thought speaking to Heba was enough. Would Heba's parents have to lie for me?

The next day at university, Heba asked me if I'd talked to Baba about going to the fake wedding with her.

"He said he needs to confirm with one of your parents."

"Oh, that's fine He can speak to my mum. She's cool and she'll be your alibi," Heba said nonchalantly.

"Really?" I asked, surprised.

"Yeah, she's always saying you should get out more and have some fun."

Even Heba's mum agreed that my life sucked.

I gave Heba Baba's number, feeling excited and worried. I might actually get away with this. But what if Baba saw through the lie?

Heba's mother called that evening.

"How are you, Um Heba?" Baba asked. "How is Heba's father?"

I couldn't hear what Heba's mum was saying on the other end of the line but Baba was staying silent and letting her talk.

"No problem *inshallah*. We'll let Heba know."

After he ended the call, he sat silently for several minutes. I didn't say a word. I was scared that if I said anything, he'd say no.

Finally, after what felt like forever, he turned to me and said, "*Tayyeb*, okay, you can go."

"Thank you, Baba!" I exclaimed, and rushed to the bathroom to pull out my phone from my bra and tell Heba this amazing news.

Now for the next hurdle—what was I going to wear? I had a few long gowns, which were the respectable thing to wear to a female-only wedding, but I couldn't wear wedding attire to a 21st birthday party. All the girls would be wearing short dresses or little tops and miniskirts, and they'd look sexy. I had none of those.

"Don't you worry," Heba told me the next day as we walked to our lecture together. "We're the same size, you can wear something of mine. I'll help you with your make-up and hair too!"

Friday rolled around and I packed an overnight bag. I put a long, lilac strapless gown into the bag along with a pair of glittery gold high heels, in case my parents wanted to see my outfit.

Heba arrived at two o'clock, honking the horn of her navy-blue BMW for the whole street to hear. Baba, Mum and my brothers were at the dining table eating falafel sandwiches, like they did every Friday after *jum'ah* prayer, but Saffa was eating her falafel sandwich in her bedroom.

Ever since Baba had slapped her repeatedly over the mobile phone fiasco, she'd confined herself to her bedroom, not wanting to speak to Baba or Abdullah.

"Heba's outside. See you all tomorrow *inshallah*," I said, standing at the doorway of the dining room.

"Have fun," Mum said.

Baba didn't look up from his falafel sandwich.

I went outside, closed the front door behind me and got into Heba's car. She squealed with excitement.

"Happy birthday, love!" I said, giving her a hug and a big kiss on the cheek, and then I gave her a birthday gift—a pair of silver earrings, which had cost me a whole month's pocket money.

"I'm so excited you're coming to my party tonight!" she said, holding both of my hands in hers and shaking them. "Let's get going, I have lots of things I need to sort out."

Once we got to her house, a villa in a compound that was inhabited mainly by Western expats, her mother opened the door and gave me a gigantic hug.

Heba took me to her bedroom, which had an en-suite bathroom and a walk-in closet that was bigger than mine and Saffa's rooms put together. She was the only child and her parents had given her the biggest bedroom in the villa.

"Right, we need to figure out what you're going to wear," she said, walking into her closet.

I joined her and looked at the numerous rows of tops, skirts and dresses, which she had arranged by colour. She had enough clothes to fill a shop. There was shelf after shelf of jeans and at least a hundred pairs of shoes. Honestly, I didn't know where to start.

"I think as my newly-appointed stylist you should pick something out for me," I said. "I don't know what suits me."

Heba pulled out several short dresses, miniskirts and tops and laid them out on her king-size bed. We didn't share the same shoe size, so whatever we chose for me to wear had to go with my glittery gold heels. I tried on a nude bodycon dress, which on her flattered her hourglass figure with her perfect flat tummy so that she looked like Sofia Vergara, but when I put it on I looked like the Michelin man. I tried sucking in my tummy, but to no avail.

Next I tried on a black miniskirt with a strappy black top that had gold beading, but the straps made my flabby arms look huge. It was third time lucky when I tried on a black dress that had long sleeves and sheer panels down the sides and on the back. It was short, only reaching the middle of my thighs, but it wasn't too tight and I felt that for a short dress it was relatively modest, the sheer panels making it alluring at the same time.

"You look hot!" Heba said, making me twirl around. "If I was a guy I'd hit on you!"

I laughed. I took the dress off and put my long-sleeved T-shirt and denim maxi skirt back on, along with my *hijab*, so we could go downstairs and eat the late lunch her mother had prepared for us.

My outfit was sorted, Heba would be doing my hair and make-up later, and she'd managed to borrow one of her friend's ID cards. A friend whose features weren't too different to my own. Cinderella was going to the ball!

Like Heba, I had long, dark brown curly hair, but unlike Heba, I wasn't proud of my curls. My entire life, I'd never felt a connection to Baba's homeland. When people asked me where I was from, I'd emphasise that I was British, and leave out the Egyptian part. Even the Arabic dialect I spoke wasn't his Egyptian dialect, it was Gulf Arabic. So when Heba tried her hardest to convince me to leave my hair curly for her party, and offered to put some curl-forming mousse in it, I was having none of it. In the end she sighed, gave up, and took out her straighteners.

We spent another hour doing each other's make-up and then we realised we were starting to run late, so we panicked and hurriedly changed into our party dresses.

Heba looked like a Hollywood star. She wore a gold bodycon dress which showed off her long tanned legs, with a push-up bra that exposed the top of her perfectly tanned breasts, nude Louboutin platform heels, and a gold knuckle-duster clutch. Her beautiful, brown curls cascaded down her back. I didn't get how she was still single.

I wasn't sure about how I looked. Heba made me pose while she took pictures with her phone. She kept saying how beautiful and sexy I looked, but when I took a glance at myself in her floor-length mirror, I didn't see it. I just saw a white girl—with dark hair and facial features that were neither completely English nor fully Arab—who was trying too hard.

I put on my black *abaya* and wrapped my black chiffon

shayla loosely around my head so my hair wouldn't get messed up. Her parents were cuddled up on the sofa watching TV downstairs in the living room.

We walked noisily down the stairs in our high heels, and her parents turned around to take a look at us. Once we had made it all the way downstairs and into the entrance of the living room, her mother stood up, walked over to us and started making a fuss.

"Two moons!" she exclaimed in Arabic, making us both twirl for her. "May Allah protect you both and allow me to celebrate at both of your weddings!"

I wondered what Baba would have thought of what I was wearing. I could just imagine Baba's look of shame and disgust. *Sharmootah*!

Birthday Girl

We arrived at the five-star hotel where the bar was located just after 9pm. At the entrance of the hotel, two Indian men dressed in a uniform of long-sleeved white blouses with billowing sleeves, gold waistcoats and red harem pants, like something out of *Aladdin*, opened our car doors.

Heba handed one of them her car keys so they could valet her car. My heart was beating like crazy inside my ribcage. I felt a little sweaty. I couldn't stop thinking that someone in the hotel lobby would know Baba and recognise me.

We walked through the lobby. Heba was graceful in her Louboutins, while I tottered along, not used to my heels. I'd only worn them a few times and was always worried I'd trip over the ends of my *abaya*.

When we got to the lift, we pressed the button that would take us to the bar on the top floor.

"Take off your *abaya* and *shayla*. We can leave them with one of the hotel staff at the door of the bar," Heba said.

I took them off, and the middle-aged Arab couple who were standing inside the elevator with us looked at me disapprovingly.

I looked in the other direction, pretending I hadn't noticed them staring, but I felt my chest tighten.

Heba handed me her friend's ID card and I put it inside my clutch. The middle-aged couple got out of the lift a couple of floors later and I felt myself relax.

Once the lift had reached the top floor, we stepped out and I could feel the vibrations of the music coming from the direction of the bar. There were so many people talking, laughing and clinking their glasses.

Heba sauntered over to a high table, where an employee stood with a laptop and hand scanner. I stayed close behind her.

"I have a reservation here for forty people for my birthday party under the name of Heba."

So many people! I hadn't realised Heba had that many friends. I could count all my friends on two hands.

The employee, an Eastern European woman, checked the list of reservations on her laptop.

"Can I have your IDs please?" she requested.

Heba went first, casually handing over her ID card, which the woman put through the scanner that was connected to a government portal. The portal kept track of everyone who passed through bars and nightclubs in the country. It was then my turn to hand over the ID card that didn't belong to me. Trying to look as cool as possible, I handed it over, and she put it through the scanner and handed it back to me. She didn't even check it!

"Do you mind if I leave these with you and pick them up on my way out?" I asked the hotel employee, signalling to my now rolled up *abaya* and *shayla*.

"Not at all," she replied and she motioned at me to hand

them over where she carefully hung them on the coat rail behind her. "You're the first ones to arrive." She led us inside.

Heba's friends—all from various Arab countries—were running on Arab time. They probably wouldn't arrive for another half an hour or so.

Another employee, a tall and skinny Kenyan man, greeted us and showed us to our table. It was rooftop bar, surrounded by glass panels with a breath-taking view of the city. Circular white tables were dotted around the bar, each one encircled by matching white, square, leather seats.

A hip-looking Arab guy with long hair tied in a low bun, a straggly moustache and beard, and round sunglasses (yes, sunglasses at night) worked the decks at the DJ booth that sat on an elevated stage.

The bar was filling up with groups of young Arab men and women. The men had oily, slicked-back hair and wore tight shirts, leaving two or three buttons open at the top, exposing their thick, dark, chest hair. The women wore dresses that were too tight for them with muffin tops bulging unattractively. Many of them had dyed blonde hair and heavy make-up.

Balding middle-aged English and American men sat on stools at the bar, perving on groups of young East Asian women who were enjoying a night off from working as air stewardesses.

I stood nervously beside our table, which had a silver bucket filled with ice holding a large bottle of vodka, as well as cranberry juice, orange juice and various soft drinks. I took in all these sights around me, feeling very out of place. I felt like someone would realise that I'd never been to a bar or mixed freely with men before.

It was an hour later when the first of Heba's friends turned up. I only knew two of her friends who had been in high school with me. Heba was a social butterfly, trying to give everybody an equal amount of attention, so I stuck with the two girls I knew.

After a while Heba came up to me and gently nudged me.

"You have to mingle. Come on, I'll introduce you to everyone!" She yanked me by the hand and started introducing me to the group. Many of her friends were also Egyptian.

"Do you want to open the bottle of vodka?" a bartender asked.

"Yes please! Anyone want to order?" Heba asked.

Heba's friends crowded around the table, each making requests for vodka and juice, or vodka and Red Bull.

"What would you like?" the bartender asked me.

"Oh, just 7Up please."

"You don't want to try just a sip of vodka?" Heba asked, offering me her glass.

"No, no, I'm fine with soft drinks, thank you," I replied.

The thought of drinking alcohol both intrigued and scared me. Mum had told me so many horror stories of girls drinking, blacking out and waking up the next day to discover they'd been raped. The idea of drinking something that would remove my inhibitions made me shudder. Plus, drinking alcohol is *haram* and it felt like a step too far.

As 11 o'clock approached, the bar was bursting to the brim with dancing bodies, and the music had changed from the melodic and soothing beats of deep house to banging dancefloor fillers.

Heba and her friends were getting tipsy and had started grinding on one another.

Someone cried out, "Shots!" and they all cheered as the bartender came back with a circular tray crammed with shot glasses coated in salt crystals with a lime wedge perched on each one.

Everyone took a shot glass and Heba shouted, "One, two, three!" before they all downed their shots together, sucking on their lime wedges, before grimacing at each other and laughing.

I just stood there pretending to look amused when really I felt completely isolated. I was starting to regret my decision about coming to Heba's birthday party, and wished I was in the comfort of my bedroom, reading a book or listening to music on my MP3 player.

And the dress! Every time I moved I felt the dress riding up my thighs and I'd try to pull it back down as subtly as I could. I felt the eyes of men from across the bar boring into me and I didn't like it.

"Hey, why are you sulking over there? Come and dance with us!" one of Heba's guy friends said. He was bald, with small square glasses, a neat moustache and beard. In his hand he held a brown ceramic smoking pipe, which he puffed on every so often.

He seemed friendly so I smiled and joined him. The others cheered as I joined the circle they'd formed, dancing to Bruno Mars.

At first, I swayed a little from side to side. Did a little shuffling of my feet. Then, Heba came over and joined us, and took both my hands in hers. It was as if she could sense my uneasiness and I finally loosened up. I started dancing the way I did in the privacy of my bedroom, in my underwear late at night, with my earphones in.

"Look at you!" exclaimed Heba, and she clapped.

For the first time in a really long time, I started to have fun. I shimmied up to the bearded guy with the pipe and the music suddenly changed to Hip-Hop. The girls in the group went mental as the DJ played *Low* by Flo Rida, holding their glasses of vodka up high and grinding on one another.

Heba was dancing with one of her guy friends, who was trying to hold his drink out of the way, spilling it on his shoes in the process. When the Hip-Hop music blared from the speakers I didn't know what to do with myself. I certainly wasn't going to start grinding on a man I'd just met five minutes ago!

"I'm going to get a drink," I said and Heba's friend smiled at me. I wasn't sure if he heard me over the loud music.

I ordered another 7Up, sat down and sipped it as I moved my hair to one side. Even though the weather at night was cooler and there was a gentle breeze, all the dancing and the heat of the bodies around me meant my neck had started to sweat, and once that happened, my hair started to frizz up. Curly hair problems.

From the safety of my chair I watched Heba and her friends. Heba was getting more and more drunk, and was now sitting on the lap of a young Arab man at the next table. One of Heba's girlfriends noticed and pulled Heba up.

As midnight approached, our bartender came out with a huge birthday cake in the shape of a Chanel bag, topped with a sparkler, and the DJ played a club remix of 'Happy Birthday.' Everyone in the bar watched as the cake made its way to our table and we all sang. The sparkler went out and everybody cheered.

Just as I began to tuck into my second slice of birthday cake,

I heard a retching sound, and looked up to see Heba with her head in the empty ice bucket vomiting.

I put the cake down and took her by the arm, along with another one of her girlfriends, and we led her across the bar to the ladies' toilets. She went into a cubicle and continued to vomit. I followed her in and held her hair out of the way.

"You came with Heba, right?" asked the girl. "Can you drive her back?"

"I don't know how to drive," I replied, and I suddenly panicked as I realised Heba was drunk and couldn't drive us. How on earth would we get back to her place?

"Okay, not a problem, we can ask the hotel to order a cab for you both and we can pick up Heba's car tomorrow morning," her friend said, and I sighed, relieved.

It was 2am and time for the bar to close. Heba's male friends chipped in to pay for the table and drinks, not allowing any of the women at the table to pay. As modern and liberal as they were, they still held the Arab view that women shouldn't pay.

I almost forgot to take my *abaya* and *shayla* back from the staff at the bar entrance, and remembered just as we were about to take the lift down. Heba's friend and I led Heba downstairs, where we ordered a cab. Within five minutes, a white Audi was waiting for us outside, and Heba and I piled into the car.

The ride home felt like it lasted forever; I was exhausted and just wanted to climb into a bed and sleep. I rarely stayed up this late. Heba was already fast asleep, and I had to pull the equivalent of £20 out of her clutch to pay the driver, as her birthday present had left me broke.

I gently woke her up when we'd reached her house, and put my arm around her to help her to the front door. I took the key out of her clutch and opened the door while she leaned her head against my shoulder. Her parents were fast asleep in their bedroom, so I had to quietly help her up the stairs, and lie her down on her bed. I took off her Louboutins, but left her dress on.

I took my own heels off, the soles of my feet blistered from wearing them for so many hours, and changed into the *jalabiyya* I'd packed in my overnight bag. I climbed into Heba's bed beside her, my ears still ringing from the loud music. It took me a while to drift off to sleep. My brain was still wired as I replayed the night's events over and over in my head, still amazed that I'd been able to pull of such a risky feat and go to a real, grown-up party.

Fahad

I went to a party. A party in a bar with boys! And I didn't get caught by Baba. I could hardly believe it.

"My friends love you, by the way," Heba said, as we walked into university. "And the guys asked me why I've been hiding such a beautiful friend."

"Really?" I asked, blushing.

Heba linked arms with me. "Told you it's fun to go out!"

Heba's friends added me on Facebook and started to invite me to their parties. I couldn't get away with going to parties every weekend without my parents getting suspicious, plus we were in our final year of university. I had dissertations to write and exams to study for.

But once a month, I'd tell Baba there was a Gulf wedding I'd been invited to and he would let me go with Heba. The story that I was going to someone's engagement party or wedding was a plausible one because in the Gulf it was normal for the young women my age to get married within weeks of each other.

In the mid-2000s most Arab women got married while they were at university or soon after graduating. Plus, agreeing to

Heba picking me up meant Baba saved himself having to drive me places. It was the perfect arrangement.

Sometimes Heba would drop me home afterwards, and if Baba was in a very good mood, he'd let me sleep over at hers. I started to feel like I was leading a double life and I wasn't bad at it.

Despite all the new-found interest from the Egyptian guys in Heba's circle, I wasn't interested in any of them. I was still attracted to Gulf men, despite that weird date I went on months ago. I'd written my date with Aziz off as a one-off.

Unlike the other expatriate girls I knew who went out with them just to get free expensive dinners, rides in sports cars and lavish gifts, it wasn't the Gulf men's wealth that attracted me.

I can admit I was a bit of a romantic, and found their Arab beauty alluring. I also felt that their lives, as boring and as routine as they were, had a sense of stability I hadn't felt all my life. My childhood memories were of us moving from area to area in London. Even now, in the Gulf, I still felt a sense of insecurity, knowing that at any time if the government wanted to, they could terminate Baba's work visa and we'd be deported.

I didn't want to have to move again. I just wanted to settle down in one place, and Gulf families spent their whole lives in the Gulf. I believed that somehow, if I could find a good Gulf guy, we'd fall in love and he'd do the honourable thing and ask Baba for my hand in marriage.

One evening I was sitting on the family computer, browsing through an Arabic entertainment website, when I saw a banner ad for an Islamic marriage website. I looked over my shoulders to make sure no one was around. Mum was downstairs cooking and Baba was having a nap. Saffa and Abdullah were in their rooms studying, and God knows where Ahmed was. He was always out in the evenings, and neither Mum nor Baba asked him where he was and what he was up to. He was free to come and go as he pleased.

I clicked on the banner ad and it took me to the website. The home page had stock photos of smiling Muslim couples holding hands or putting their arms around one another. The membership was free.

I signed up, attaching one of the few photos I'd saved on the computer. It was me wearing my *abaya* and *shayla*, with a full face of make-up that Heba had taken for a photography project.

I knew Baba had showed that picture to his friends who had sons, much to my protest. After a year of me refusing all marriage proposals, he'd given up and now told anyone who proposed that I wasn't interested in getting married.

Don't get me wrong, I did want to get married, just not to one of his backward *salafi* friends' sons. I didn't want my life dictated by misogynistic doctrines that believed that women should go to university, but then get married as soon as they graduated, hang their degree up on the living room wall like a decorative painting, focus on the housework, pop out babies and get dinner ready for when their husband came home from work. No thank you.

So, after setting up my profile on the Islamic marriage website, I decided to set my filters so only Gulf men's profiles appeared. I clicked 'Search' and hundreds of profiles swept on to the computer screen.

I went through profile after profile, until I couldn't search anymore. I logged out, then cleared the Internet history. I didn't want my parents or Abdullah stumbling across this website and figuring out that it was me.

I logged on again the next evening and found dozens of Arabic messages in my inbox, mostly from Egyptian men or men with faces that only their mothers could love. But in the midst of them I found a message from a Gulf guy who went to my university.

In his profile picture he was sitting on a jet ski, smiling at the camera, and had really cute dimples. The message was in English. Score! Someone who actually speaks English.

I think you have a very interesting profile. You write that you're British but I can see that you have Arab features. I think you're beautiful. My name is Fahad. I'd love to have a coffee with you. If you're interested, this is my number.

I wrote down his number on the inside of my arm and pulled my sleeve down, then logged out of the website, cleared the Internet history and went to the bathroom. I pulled Heba's mobile out of my bra and added his number to my contacts. I wasted no time and sent him a text message in English.

ME: *Hi, this is Sara from the marriage website.*

He replied almost straight away.

FAHAD: *Hala walla! I'm so glad you've texted me. I've been thinking about you all day, hoping you'd see my message.*

ME: *So about your offer for a coffee? I'd love to. Only thing is I'd need you to pick me up from the guys' car park at uni and then drop me off back there. I can't be picked up or dropped off anywhere near my house.*

FAHAD: *Totally understandable. Have you got any free periods at uni tomorrow? I've only got lectures in the morning then I'm free from lunchtime.*

I had lectures all day. I was sure I could skip the afternoon ones and get away with it. I was really careful not to skip the same lectures too often. Plus, one of them was Professor Munthir's and he was always cool.

ME: *Yeah I can do lunchtime. See you at the guys' car park at 12pm?*

FAHAD: *Done. Can't wait to see you!*

ME: *Can't wait to see you too!*

When it came to dating Gulf guys I didn't have to explain myself to them. They knew I couldn't call them at home while Baba or Abdullah were around. They got it when I said I couldn't be dropped off outside my house. It worked both ways. They wouldn't be able to tell their parents about me, nor could I tell my parents about them. But there were double standards. These Gulf guys still dated in secret but if they caught their own sisters talking to a guy they'd beat them up and put them under house arrest.

At midday, Fahad was waiting for me in the guys' car park

in his black Mercedes E-Class and he looked just as cute as he had in his picture.

I hopped into his car, the end of my *shayla* covering my face.

"You don't need to be covering your face with a *ghishwa*," Fahad said. He had an American accent.

"Maybe I should, just till we get to wherever it is we're going? I'm worried someone who knows me and my dad will see me," I replied.

Fahad shrugged and smiled. "That's cool with me. I won't ever tell you to cover your face though, like other Gulf guys."

We zoomed through the security barriers without a second glance from the security guards. I was more confident about going out with a guy from university now.

"What's your favourite cuisine?" Fahad asked as we sped down the highway.

"I dunno, no one's ever asked me that question before. Italian maybe?"

"Awesome, Italian's my favourite too. I know the perfect little place run by actual Italians in the *souq*. Let's go there."

The *souq* was a bazaar fashioned on the traditional market places of Arabia hundreds of years ago. It was full of fascinating little shops selling all sorts: antiques, carpets, kitchenware, even pets! A mix of the past and the present, nestled in between the shops were small restaurants offering a range of world cuisines. I walked along the cobbled pathways in wonder, feeling like Princess Jasmine in *Aladdin* when she escapes for the first time to the market from the palace disguised as a common woman.

My date with Fahad was everything that my date with Aziz wasn't. The Italian restaurant was small and rustic.

"How comes you have an American accent?" I asked Fahad as we were served our chicken fettuccine alfredo.

"I watched a lot of American movies and shows growing up," he replied after finishing his first mouthful of food. "And I spend every summer at our house in Chelsea in London. That's why my English is so good, even though I never went to an international school."

Unlike Aziz, Fahad got all my jokes and all my references Western music, TV shows and movies. When I spoke to him about places in London he knew what I was talking about. It was perfect. A Gulf guy I actually connected with.

Majlis

Over the next couple of weeks, Fahad and I went on more dates on the days I finished early from uni and had enough time to be dropped back in time for the five o'clock bus.

After three weeks of dating, the furthest we'd gone physically was holding hands while he drove the car. He'd have one hand on the steering wheel and his other hand holding mine, our fingers interlocked. I was relieved he hadn't tried to go any further. It hadn't taken me long to become smitten and he was already calling me his *habibah*, the Arabic word for girlfriend.

When I was at home, we contacted each other via text message, and every time I saw him, he'd give me a top-up card with more phone credit.

One evening, he sent me a text asking me to come to his house for lunch and to play video games in the *majils*. The *majils* is the part of a Gulf family's house where only male family members and their friends are allowed to hang out. They chat, play cards, eat and play video games.

His invitation sounded innocent enough and so I accepted.

FAHAD: *So what are you going to tell your dad?*

ME: *I'll say I'm at a friend's house studying and having dinner. That way I don't have to rush back to university to catch the bus. But how are you going to sneak me into the majlis?*

FAHAD: *Oh don't worry about that. It's a separate building so no one will see you. I'll have it sorted.*

I was going to take a big risk and have him drop me off home, not too close to the house, probably a few streets away from it, so that the neighbours wouldn't see me.

Now I just needed to ask Baba for permission to be out after university the next day. I'd only been out three days ago over the weekend, at one of Heba's friends' parties, so I wasn't sure how he'd react to a request to go out again so soon, even if it was on the premise of studying.

I went downstairs to see what kind of mood he was in. He wasn't in the living room, and I could hear water running in the ground floor bathroom, so I assumed he was in there making *wudu*, the ritual washing Muslims make before praying.

I perched myself nervously on the edge of the sofa, barely listening to the TV. Baba walked into the living room towards the crockery cabinet, where he'd left his glasses and watch.

"I didn't know you enjoyed watching Faisal Al-Qasim. I think it's time he went to Turkey like all the other Al Jazeera presenters and invested in a hair transplant," Baba said grinning, as he buttoned up his shirt cuffs.

I pretended to find his joke amusing and faked a loud laugh. He seemed to be in a good mood.

"Baba, can I go to Heba's house tomorrow to study?"

"Didn't you just see her a few days ago when you went to that engagement party? I think you're going out too much these days," he replied, fastening his watch to his wrist.

"We have midterms coming up and I don't know how to do some of the calculations in our Principles of Finance module. She's really good at maths. She helped me pass our last quiz."

I'd become a really good liar, almost pathological. He looked me straight in the eye.

Finally he said, "Go, and I better see you with an A for this module."

"*Shukran*, thank you Baba," I said, and leapt up to go to the bathroom so I could text Fahad.

He was going to pick me up at lunchtime from the men's campus, and I was going to lie to my professor and say that I needed to go home because I had an upset stomach.

Fahad wasn't like the other Gulf guys I'd heard about from the women at university. He didn't ask me to cover my face when I was with him, or to walk ten steps behind him so no one would see us together. He worked out at the gym and had broad shoulders and bulging biceps that made his *thowb* sleeves just a little too tight for him. He wore his *ghutra* wrapped loosely around his head, not all prim and precise like most other Gulf guys, whose *ghutras* were starched and pointed. He just threw both ends of the *ghutra* over his *egaal* like he didn't give it any thought.

He'd told me many times that he didn't like wearing the *thowb* and *ghutra*, and he preferred Western clothes, but his father told him it wasn't manly not to wear the *thowb*.

"You should wear whatever you want," I said.

"My dad doesn't get it," Fahad replied, shaking his head. "He said it's our customs and traditions. As long as he's putting a roof over my head I have no freedom of choice."

I hadn't realised that guys here could be trapped too. They definitely had more freedom than the girls—they could go out whenever and wherever they liked—but they were still expected to obey all their fathers' wishes.

As we left the vicinity of the university in Fahad's car and stopped at a traffic light, he turned to me and said, "We're going to need to stop off somewhere quiet and get you to wear one of my *thowbs* and a *ghutra*."

"What?" I laughed. "You're joking, right?"

But he didn't laugh with me. "That's how we're getting you into the *majlis*."

"Come on! No one's going to see me sitting beside you and believe I'm a man."

"Just trust me. You do trust me?" Fahad asked.

"Of course I do," I replied quietly.

Fahad drove the car into an area which was populated with run-down, one-level houses. They were once occupied by the grandparents of today's rich generation who had left when they acquired their oil wealth. They built grand mansions elsewhere. These neglected traditional Arabic houses—which had open courtyards in their centre—were now inhabited by poor South Asian labourers. The beige cement walls were decorated with graffiti in Urdu, English, Hindi and Arabic.

Fahad pulled into a quiet alleyway. "Climb over to the back seat." He went to the boot and passed through a white *thowb* and *ghutra* along with a black *egaal*.

"Take off your *abaya* and *shayla* and put them in your bag, and then put the *thowb* on over your clothes," he instructed.

The *thowb* was far too big for me and swallowed up my arms. I climbed back into the front seat and he got into the driver's seat. He tried his best to tuck my hair into a skullcap and then arranged the *ghutra* over that. He handed me his dark aviator sunglasses to wear and wrapped one end of the *ghutra* over my nose and mouth. On me his sunglasses were so big that they covered half my face.

"You look like a Bedouin now. Look in the mirror!" he said, laughing.

I pulled down the car sun visor and opened the sliding mirror. I looked ridiculous.

"You can still see that I'm a woman!" I protested.

"No you can't!" he said. "It will be fine."

As we got near his house, another car driving in the opposite direction slowed down beside us. A middle-aged Gulf man had his window wound all the way down and he looked at me and then looked at Fahad, squinting with confusion drawn all over his face, and then he drove off. Fahad found this hilarious and burst out laughing, while I was absolutely terrified the man was going to stop the car and question us because he thought we were a gay couple.

Fahad pulled into the driveway directly outside the one-floor annex that was the *majlis*. It was a separate building to the house. I couldn't see into it because its long glass windows had been tinted.

"Get out of the car quickly and shut the car door quietly," he said.

He took the *majlis* key out of his pocket, unlocked the door and we went inside. As soon as I was in, he quickly scrambled to lock the door from the inside.

The *majlis* was pretty traditional. Sturdy red and black Bedouin floor cushions formed an L shape around the fully carpeted room, and a giant flat-screen TV stood to one side. Two PlayStation handsets lay strewn on the floor. There was a low-lying glass-top coffee table in the middle of the room, which was laden with bowls of *Celebrations* chocolates. The *majlis* had an en-suite bathroom too.

"Are you hungry? We usually eat lunch here at two or three, and it's only one, but if the food is ready I can have the maid bring it in," Fahad asked.

"I'm a bit hungry," I replied.

"Okay, wait here, and our maid Nancy will bring it in."

I frowned. "Err, if Nancy sees me isn't she going to snitch on you to your parents?"

"No, don't worry, Nancy's cool. My brother brings girls here all the time."

I looked at the long, flat, floor cushion I was sitting on and wondered how many hook-ups had taken place on it.

"You can take off the *thowb* now by the way," Fahad said, and smiled, before turning around, leaving the *majlis* and locking the door quietly behind him.

He came back several minutes later with Nancy, their petite twenty-something Filipina maid, who was carrying a large round metal tray with a giant lid, smoke billowing out from its sides. She was wearing a servant's uniform, consisting of a lilac smock with white buttons down the centre, and matching lilac trousers. Her straight black hair was scraped back into a bun.

I didn't see why Fahad couldn't have brought the food in himself. He was carrying two small pots of plain white yoghurt and a little plate of salad while she carried a tray that was almost as big as she was.

"Hello madam," she said in a meek voice, as she knelt down precariously, trying to keep her balance as she laid the tray down on the floor.

Fahad didn't even offer to take it off her. I felt bothered by this. This fully grown man who worked out at the gym wouldn't lift a finger to help. After Nancy scurried out, Fahad locked the door behind her. He took off his white *ghutra* and crocheted skullcap, draping them over the side of a floor cushion, and then he pulled his *thowb* over his head, leaving on just his white vest, called a *faneela*, and white cotton trousers that Gulf men wore under their *thowbs* called *sirwaal*.

I'd seen men dressed in their undergarments like this on TV in Gulf soap operas, and they usually sported a pot belly, which they called a *karsh*. But Fahad had no *karsh* and he made his *faneela* and *sirwaal* look sexy.

"Let's eat," he said as he sat down cross-legged on the carpet and patted the floor, motioning at me to sit beside him.

He lifted the heavy metal lid off the tray, revealing a huge mound of chicken *kabsa*. *Kabsa* was the national dish consisting of rice and either chicken, fish or lamb cooked with lots of spices like cardamom and cloves.

"The secret is to put a bit of yoghurt on the rice and eat it."

I looked at the spread on the floor. "Fahad, you didn't bring spoons."

"You don't need a spoon! Use your fingers like me," he replied, and he showed me how with his thumb, forefinger and middle finger how to mould a ball out of rice, before popping it into his mouth.

"Yeah, I don't think I can do that," I said, dropping rice grains all over my lap as I tried unsuccessfully to form a rice ball.

Fahad stood up, opened the *majlis* door and yelled, "Nancy! Nancy, bring a spoon!"

Nancy rushed back over to the *majlis* from the main house with a spoon and handed it to me.

"Thank you," I said.

As soon as we were done eating, Fahad unlocked the *majlis* door and yelled again for Nancy to collect the tray.

Once Nancy had gone, Fahad locked the *majlis* door, turned on the TV and sat down and started playing *FIFA* on the PlayStation.

"Do you want to play?" he asked, offering me a handset.

"I'm not really into football," I said. "Don't you have anything else? *GTA* or *Call of Duty*?"

"Oh man, sorry, I don't," he said, and then he carried on playing on his own.

He was so engrossed in his game that he didn't notice how bored I was beside him. He wasn't even trying to make conversation with me! Why had he brought me here if he was just going to play video games and ignore me?

So I decided to do something a little unlike me, something a little daring, to get his attention.

I lay with my head draped across his crossed legs and stroked the side of his face with my right hand. Then I moved on to his left earlobe and used my thumb and forefinger to gently rub his soft skin. I moved my hand down to the left side of his chest and stroked it. I felt his nipple harden through his vest.

Finally, he put his handset down on the floor and looked at me.

"What are you doing?"

"Getting your attention," I replied, before I sat on his lap, wrapping my legs around his back.

"You've got it now," he said, his voice thick.

He kissed me softly and this time I didn't freeze. I kissed him back. He ran the tips of his fingers up and down my back, sending shivers down my spine, as he alternated between sucking on my lips and tongue. I started to feel things I'd never felt before. This must be what the *Cosmopolitan* website meant when they talked about getting turned on.

He brushed his lips across my face and moved on to my ear, gently breathing warm air into it, and then he moved ever so slowly down the side of my neck. But when he tried to move further down, cupping my breasts over my blouse with his hands, I froze. I patted away his hands and hurried off his lap.

"Stop," I said. "I don't want to go any further."

"But you started it," he said, grabbing my arms and pulling me back towards him. "You've turned me on. You can't just tease me leaving me with blue balls. Come on, take off your top."

He tried his best to lift up my blouse, but I forced my hands down on his so he was unable to pull it up past my belly.

"Stop," I said, pushing him away, and then I began to cry.

"You know what those tears are called?" Fahad said, crossing his arms. "Crocodile tears."

"What? I can't believe you just said that!" I exclaimed. "These are not crocodile tears!"

Fahad sat beside me and wrapped his arms around me, so my head was nestled against his neck, my tears making little damp patches on his white vest. I inhaled the strong woody notes of his perfume.

"I'm sorry," he said. "I'd never do anything to you by force. It's just you're so sexy and you turned me on. I'd never do anything without your consent."

"It's just, I've never been with a man before," I told him, drying my eyes with my sleeve. "I haven't kissed a boy before. Well, not really."

I thought back to my experiences with Faisal and Aziz. You couldn't call those real kisses.

"Are you kidding?" he asked, surprised. "But you're from the UK. You must have had boyfriends over there?"

"No, never."

He gave me a big kiss on my cheek and hugged me harder. "You know what this place is?" he said. "It's our love *majlis*. Come on, let's get you home."

Double Standards

I had to wear Fahad's *thowb* and *ghutra* again on the way out. Once we were out of his neighbourhood, we stopped off in a quiet alleyway to put my *abaya* and *shayla* back on. Fahad took us to a McDonald's drive-through on the way home and we ate our Big Macs and fries together in the car. He kept checking up on me, making sure I was okay.

Fahad dropped me off outside a supermarket three streets down from my house and I went inside to buy a bar of chocolate, so I had a legitimate excuse to give Baba if he asked me why Heba hadn't dropped me off outside our house.

When I turned my key in the lock, I could hear men's voices coming from inside the living room. The *amus* were over for a *halaqa*, their Qur'an gathering. I opened the door to find Baba already standing behind it. He ushered me past the living room and up the stairs and then went back down to re-join them.

Once I was in the safety of my room, I pulled out Heba's mobile from my bra and texted Fahad.

Hey, I've just got home. I keep replaying our make-out session over and over in my head. I'm sorry if I scared you earlier. Let's take the physical side of things slowly.

Fahad would usually text me back within minutes but an hour later I'd received nothing.

I didn't think anything of it, and climbed into bed, telling myself that maybe he was just tired and had gone straight to bed.

The next morning, when I woke up, I expected to find a text message saying *Hey, I fell asleep. Glad you're alright*, but there were no new messages. I was starting to feel a little anxious.

I waited until I was on the university bus to try calling him. I knew it was early so when he didn't pick up the phone, I told myself he must still be asleep. By lunchtime, I still hadn't heard from him. I called again and he didn't pick up. What if something had happened to him? What if he was sick or had been in a car accident? How would I know?

I couldn't focus at all. At every opportunity I had, between lectures and on the bus home, I tried calling him, and he didn't pick up.

Fahad, where are you? Are you okay? Please reply as soon as you see this message, I'm starting to freak out. Has something happened?

Nothing. Instead of putting my phone on silent that night, I put it under my pillow on vibrate mode so I'd feel it and wake up if he texted. It took me forever to fall asleep, as I imagined all the worst-case scenarios. Fahad dying in a car accident, and me not being able to contact his family because they didn't know I existed. Fahad being sick or injured, and me being unable to visit him at the hospital, because I wasn't a family member.

He wasn't on Facebook so other than his phone number, I had no other way of contacting him. When the next day passed without hearing from him, I started to get that horrible, niggly feeling you get in your chest. Had I been ghosted?

Part of me wanted to give him the benefit of the doubt that perhaps a family crisis had arisen and he was unable to contact me because of that. There was a genuine reason for his absence and we were still a couple, but a greater part of me felt like I'd been dumped. I was so disappointed. I'd really thought Fahad was different to other Gulf guys.

Three days later I received a text message from him. I felt like my temperature had shot up by 100 degrees when I saw his name on the text message notification.

I'm really sorry, I meant to contact you sooner. I can't lie to you, you're a sweet and innocent girl. I should have told you from the beginning but I had my milcha, my Islamic marriage contract, drawn up three months ago to my cousin. I understand if you don't want to see me anymore.

I re-read the message over and over again. Each time I did I was hit with a wave of nausea. I'd technically been having an affair with someone's husband. I'd made out with a married man! I texted him back.

What you did is haram and I can't be in a relationship with a married man.

The next day I told Heba the entire saga through fits of tears.

She put her arms around me and said, "No more Gulf guys. They're all the same. They're no good for us."

"You're right. That's it. I'm done with them," I said, sniffling.

But deep down, I didn't really mean it.

"Do you ever wonder where Ahmed goes every night? Sometimes he doesn't come back until the next morning." I asked Mum.

We were watching Gok Wan giving someone a makeover on BBC Prime, the one British channel we had in the Gulf.

"Between you and me, I think he's got a girlfriend."

"He's got a what? Does Baba know this?"

"He does. He found pictures of Ahmed with the same girl on Facebook."

"And?"

"Baba said he was disappointed that Ahmed had gone off the 'right path,' but that was about it."

"No lecture? No beating? No grounding? That's not fair, Mum!"

"I told Baba that it's double standards."

"And what did he say?"

"He said I don't understand how Arabs think. A young man can clean up his act and become a good Muslim and find a wife, even if he messes around for a bit. But if a young Arab woman gets caught dating, her reputation will be ruined forever."

"Who is this girl Ahmed is seeing?"

"Some English girl in Year 13."

"Do you think they sleep together?"

"If he's out every night until the morning, what do you think? Come on Sara, don't be so naïve!"

I wanted so badly to confront Baba with this information. It wasn't fair. I was almost left behind in Cairo for being in love, and Saffa almost missed her GCSEs for talking to a boy. But I didn't want to be a troublemaker. I needed to keep Ahmed on my side if I was to carry on leading my own secret life of dates and parties. That didn't stop the inequality in the treatment between boys and girls from killing me inside.

Attack

It was the week before my final exams for the semester and the university had given us the week off as study leave. Saffa, Abdullah and Ahmed usually came home from school just before the mid-afternoon *asr* prayer and Mum would give one of them money to go to the shop to buy soft drinks and sweets.

After a month of exiling herself in her bedroom, Saffa had finally re-joined family life. She was still not on talking terms with Abdullah and only spoke to Baba if she had to.

This time it was Saffa's turn to go to the local shop, dressed in her off-white, long-sleeved, school shirt, floor-length beige skirt and her white headscarf. Like me, she'd started to wear her headscarf as soon as her period started.

"I don't get why we have to wear this piece of flipping fabric on our heads," Saffa complained to me in her bedroom in private. "Wearing a scarf on your head doesn't make you a better Muslim."

"I know, but we've been taught by our Islamic Studies teachers that it's compulsory," I replied. "Even if Baba makes it optional, we'd still get punished by Allah if we took it off."

Saffa had no idea that I'd been going to mixed parties in secret and taking my headscarf off. I felt like a hypocrite. The truth was I had stopped caring. I was twenty and I wanted to live life. I made an extra prayer every evening to Allah to forgive me, and I told myself He created me, so He would understand the struggles I was going through as a young adult with a mega strict dad. He'd forgive me.

*

I sat in the living room reading through my revision notes and Mum was in the kitchen nearby, cooking dinner. Half an hour had passed and Saffa still hadn't returned.

"Does it usually take this long to buy Pepsi and chocolate?" I asked Mum, loud enough for her to hear me from the kitchen.

"Is she still not back yet?" Mum asked, walking out of the kitchen and into the living room, drying her hands on a tea towel.

"I can go to the shop and check if she's still there if you want?" I suggested.

Just as I finished my sentence, there was a bang on the front door. It was so loud that I almost jumped out of my skin.

I rushed to the front door and looked through the peep hole. It was Saffa. I opened the door and she burst in, barely making it inside before she collapsed on to the floor. The cans of Pepsi rolled out of the bag onto the ceramic tiles.

"Saffa!" Mum cried, and she knelt down beside her and held Saffa's shoulders. "What's wrong? What's happened?"

"Somebody touched me," Saffa howled.

I didn't have to ask to know what she meant.

Forgetting my headscarf and shoes, I ran out of the front door and into the street to try and find whoever it was she was talking about. The street was empty. At this time of the day people were usually at home taking an afternoon nap.

I walked to the end of the street, knowing that if any of the neighbours saw me without my headscarf they might report it to Baba and I would have some explaining to do. I didn't see anybody. I ran back to the house where Mum was holding Saffa in her arms, both of them still sitting on the floor. Abdullah and Ahmed had come downstairs and were standing helplessly on the side of the stairs.

"Call the police," Mum said. "Saffa has been sexually assaulted."

"Call Baba from your mobile phone and tell him to come home," I told Ahmed.

Ahmed didn't react the way I expected him to. I thought he'd be the one charging out of the front door, but instead he stood there frozen.

"Call Baba now!" I shouted, but he still didn't move. He just kept staring at Saffa with his eyes wide.

"I'll call Baba," Abdullah said, breaking their silence.

I picked up the landline telephone and dialled.

"This is emergency services, what service do you need?" a woman asked in Arabic.

"The police, please," I replied.

"What is your emergency?"

"My sister has been attacked."

It didn't take long for a police car to pull up outside our house. There was still no sign of Baba. Two policemen—both Gulf men—knocked at our door. One was tall and stick thin with a moustache and goatee, and the other was short, round and fat with a big beard. They both wore black trousers that were pulled so high up that their belt buckles practically sat under their chests.

Mum had managed to get Saffa to sit beside her on the living room sofa. Saffa rested her head on Mum's shoulder and was crying silently. I went upstairs and put my *abaya* and *shayla* on over my pyjamas, and then ran back downstairs.

Stick Thin Policeman took out a small notepad and pen and Ahmed, who had finally emerged from his shock, told him what Saffa had managed to tell us through her tears. Ahmed's Arabic was better than mine.

The policemen didn't look at Saffa once. Nor did they address me or Mum. Since Baba hadn't come back home yet, Ahmed was the eldest male in the house and the policemen considered him to be our guardian until Baba returned.

"She went to the *dukaan* at 2:30pm to buy soft drinks and sweets and came home over half an hour later, crying and shaking." Ahmed stopped. *Dukaan* was the Arabic word for the corner shop. He took a deep breath and continued. "She said as she walked around the corner a South Asian man pushed her into the alleyway and. . ." He was unable to finish the sentence.

Abdullah stood by Ahmed's side, looking as if he was about to cry.

"It's okay, son." Stick Thin Policeman stopped writing and looked up from his notebook. "Let's wait for your father to return home and then we'll need to go to the station. We'll need more details."

When Baba finally arrived home, he found us sitting

solemnly with the policemen. He took one look at us and dropped his briefcase on the floor.

"What happened?" he asked.

He looked at Saffa crying in Mum's arms. I thought he was going to rush over and take Saffa into his arms, but instead he walked over to Ahmed, Abdullah and the two policemen.

"Your daughter has been sexually assaulted by a South Asian labourer," Stick Thin Policeman told him in Arabic. "Unfortunately we've had several incidents like this recently. If your daughter agrees, we'd like her to come with you to the station so we can make a full report."

"I don't want to go," Saffa cried.

"You need to go, Saffa," Baba said softly. "Otherwise they won't be able to catch this man."

It was the first time he'd spoken to Saffa so gently in months.

I walked over to Saffa and held her hand. "I'll come too. I won't leave you alone."

Saffa nodded and we followed Baba outside into his car.

"We'll meet you at the station," Stick Thin Policeman told Baba, and he and his partner, who hadn't uttered a word the entire time, went back to their police car and drove off.

Trapped

I'd never been to a police station. It looked nothing like the police stations I'd seen back in London on *EastEnders*. It was in a large villa, on a residential street, and only a couple of windows on the ground floor at the back had bars on them.

We went inside and Stick Thin Policeman was waiting for us at the reception. He led us into his office, which was full of expensive-looking brown leather sofas, and he sat in a black chair behind a massive mahogany desk.

I sat on one of the sofas next to Saffa, gripping her hand tightly, and Baba sat on a visitor's chair in front of the desk.

"I'll be making the report," Stick Thin Policeman said, again addressing Baba. He asked Baba for his and Saffa's national ID cards, and then called in a young Indian man in a waiter's waistcoat, the 'tea boy,' and told him to make photocopies. Baba wrote down our address and his contact details for the police report.

"Can you please ask your daughter to tell us exactly what happened?"

Saffa shook her head and turned to me. "Sara, I can't," she whispered.

"Can I talk on her behalf?" I asked the policeman in Arabic. "She's still too upset to talk."

"No problem," the policeman replied. "You tell us what she told you."

I told him, mustering the best Arabic I could, that a middle-aged South Asian man with a black beard and moustache, wearing a blue boiler suit, pushed my sister into the dirty alleyway beside the *dukaan* where sewage water trickled in a line over the sandy and stony ground. He pinned her against the wall. The branches and leaves from the willow tree in the front yard of the villa next door hid them from plain view of the street.

Saffa in that moment froze from shock and couldn't fight back, as he pressed his lips against hers and groped her breasts. The handles of the blue plastic bag she held tightly cut red grooves into the folds of her fingers. I told him how he slid his hand down the elastic waistband of her school skirt, into her knickers, and assaulted her with his hand for several minutes until he let her go. The whole time he didn't say a word.

When I got to the part about her knickers, Baba's face lost all of its colour.

"Why didn't you fight back?" Baba asked Saffa in English.

Saffa started to cry again. "I couldn't move. It was like I was trapped inside my body."

Stick Thin Policeman had finished typing and looked up at Baba. "Now that we have a description of him we'll send patrol cars to your local area to see if we can find anyone that fits his profile, and we'll bring anyone we suspect in for questioning.

It may be that your daughter will have to identify him from photographs. We'll call you if we have any leads."

Baba and Stick Thin Policeman stood up and shook hands. During the time we were there, I didn't see any police women. No one from the police had asked Saffa if she needed any counselling or if she was okay.

The car drive home was silent. Baba stopped at the local mosque near our house to pray *maghrib* prayer. The sun had started to set, sending brilliant pink rays across the sky. Saffa and I were sat together in the back seat, my hand in hers.

"You were very brave at the police station."

Saffa nodded, trying to blink away her tears.

When Baba had finished praying and came back to the car, he turned to Saffa. "What did you buy from the shop earlier?"

"Some cans of Pepsi and Galaxy bars," Saffa replied.

"You know Pepsi is manufactured by a Zionist company," he replied. "And we're supposed to be boycotting Zionist products. Maybe this was a punishment from God."

Saffa and I looked at each other bewildered. Was he actually serious? I was about to open my mouth but Saffa squeezed my hand tight and shook her head. For her sake I didn't say a word.

I waited until we were home and Baba had gone out to the mosque again to pray *ishaa* before telling Mum what he'd said in the car. Mum was sat on the living room sofa, holding Saffa in her arms.

"Please don't tell me this. You're just making me hate him even more." She let Saffa go and put her head between her hands. "Sara, you need to understand that I have nowhere to go if I take you kids and leave him. And that's if he lets me take you. The laws here give him the power to stop us all from travelling. I have no rights here as a married woman, and you know my family in England won't help me unless I leave Islam."

"Why don't you do it then? Just lie and tell your parents that you're leaving the religion but secretly stay Muslim. They can't remove Islam from your heart," I said.

"I'm scared." Mum looked up. "I'm scared that if I disobey my husband, if I lie and pretend to leave my religion, that Allah will punish me. Maybe this misery is a test from Allah. Maybe I just need to stay strong and Allah will reward me when I die in *jannah*."

"I don't believe Allah created us to be miserable all our lives and I definitely don't believe he will stop you from going to Heaven. If there's a way out, a way to be happy, we should take it. If your parents say they'll have us back we should take the chance. We'll still be Muslim without Baba," I argued.

"Baba will be back from the mosque any minute now," Mum said, ending our conversation. "Take Saffa upstairs."

"Come, let me take you to bed." I held out my hand to Saffa, and she rose from the sofa and took it. We quietly exited the living room while Mum muttered every swear word under the sun about Baba.

*

Mum allowed Saffa to take a week off school under the premise that she was sick. Mum and I searched for a child psychologist but unfortunately, in the mid 2000s, there was no such thing. There were psychiatrists who dealt with adults suffering from mental illnesses, but no counselling services. Mum and I had to do the counselling with Saffa ourselves.

"None of this is your fault," we repeated over and over to Saffa. "Don't let Baba make you think otherwise."

If Saffa was withdrawn before, now she didn't even speak. I'd talk to her and be met with silence. She was losing weight. Most days the only meal she ate was the sandwich Mum made for her packed lunch.

Saffa didn't speak to anyone for a whole month. The first words she said when she broke her silence were around the dinner table one evening where she looked at Baba and said, "I don't want to wear the *hijab* anymore."

I expected Baba to say something, but he sat in silence staring at Saffa.

"You said that wearing the *hijab* would protect me, and it didn't," Saffa said.

Baba looked down at his plate and didn't say a word.

The next day, Saffa went to school minus her headscarf. A few days later she cut her hair into a short bob with a short straight fringe, and then she dyed it black with one of those home box dye kits. Still Baba didn't say anything.

Mum joked that she looked like a goth. Unlike me, Saffa was blessed with Mum's English hair genes, and with her straight hair, her new hairstyle made her look like Emily the Strange.

Saffa seemed to have taken Mum's comment literally because she took on a new gothic persona completely. Apart from when the *amus* were over and we were strictly forbidden from being seen or heard, she would play heavy metal, blaring bands like HIM, Evanescence and Lacuna Coil. None of us had dared to play English music out loud.

"Sara, tell Saffa to turn that music down. She'll attract

demons and djinns to the house," Baba said, as we sat in the living room while Saffa's music blared from upstairs.

I was gobsmacked that he was allowing heavy metal, a genre of music that conservative Muslims associated with devil worshipping, to be played out loud.

He may not have openly admitted it, but I believe his new-found leniency with Saffa was his way of saying he was sorry for how he'd behaved with her.

Release

Upstairs, Mum and Baba had an en-suite bathroom, but my siblings and I shared one bathroom. Ahmed, Abdullah and I started having to schedule slots for quick showers in the mornings. For the past few months, Saffa started to spend two or three hours every evening in there having a bath.

"I need the toilet!" Ahmed yelled, banging his fist on the door. "What are you doing in there? It's been two hours!"

Another half hour later Saffa would walk out casually without a word.

"Mum, would you have a word with Saffa please?" I pleaded as Mum prepared my siblings' packed lunches. "We can't go on like this without access to the bathroom for three hours every evening."

"I'll see what's going on," Mum replied without looking up from her sandwich-making.

Later that evening, I was sitting on my bed doing my university reading when Mum came into my room looking like she had seen a ghost and sat down beside me. I put down my textbook.

"What's wrong?" I asked her.

"Did you know Saffa is self-harming?" Mum asked quietly.

I gasped. I had no idea. It's considered *haram* in Islam to inflict harm on yourself. Self-harm was something I'd read about in magazines, but I'd never known anyone in real life who had done it, let alone my little sister.

"No I didn't! Wait, are you sure? How do you know?"

"Saffa came to me early this morning—you'd already left for university—and she rolled up her shirt sleeve. She had a blood-soaked bandage wrapped around her left arm. She's been using the blades from Baba's razors to cut herself every evening in the bath, and last night she cut too deep and bled throughout the night. She didn't even come to me when it happened. She could have bled to death while we all slept! She said she almost fainted, yet she didn't think to come to one of us for help!" Mum rubbed her forehead with the back of her hand as if she was in pain.

"Does Baba know?" I asked, in a shaky voice.

"Not yet." Mum sighed. "I kept her off school and took her to the primary healthcare centre and they had to give her stitches. You know here if they think you're trying to commit suicide they'll contact the police, so I told them it was an accident."

"Did they not notice other cuts?"

"Well if they did they didn't ask."

I swallowed several times to keep myself from crying. I knew that if I started, I would set Mum off, and it was clear from the pained look on her face that she was just about holding herself together. Plus I didn't want Ahmed or Abdullah to walk past my room and hear us sobbing, and cause them any upset. It was starting to feel like our lives were full of distress.

We all wore our long sleeve *jalabiyyas* at home and I hadn't noticed any cuts or scars on Saffa's arms. I was angry with myself for not having picked up on any signs.

"I've got a plan that doesn't need my parents or us denouncing our religion," Mum confided in me.

"Okay, this sounds promising, what is it?" I asked.

"I'll lie and tell Baba my mum is dying and that it's our last chance to see her and I need you for moral support. I'll say I want to take Saffa so she can have a break from everything that's happened to her."

"You can't lie about Grandma dying! That's an awful thing to lie about," I said.

"Ssshh, wait, let me carry on," Mum said. "We'll go to England and I'll find us a women's refuge and make arrangements. I'll tell them my husband was abusive so we had to leave."

"And what about Ahmed and Abdullah?"

"Once we've been housed somewhere by the council they'll be able to come back if they want to."

So many things could go wrong. For one, would Baba even believe her story about my grandmother dying? Would he agree to Saffa and I going along with her? What if we got back to England and we had to wait years for a council flat? I didn't say anything though, because if having a plan gave Mum hope, I wasn't going to take it away from her.

"Are you going to tell Baba about Saffa?" I asked.

"I'll have to," she replied. "I want him to know how unhappy we all are. She could have died last night, Sara. She's traumatised after the sexual assault and there's no help for her here. Whoever did this to her, he's gotten away with it. I hope he rots in hell for what he did. I can't even tell the poor girl they haven't found him so they're now closing the case."

"Are you serious? That's not fair! They need to keep looking for him."

"It's been a month Sara," Mum said sadly. "There's nothing we can do."

A day later, as I sat on my bed revising for my exams, I heard a quiet knock on my bedroom door.

"Come in," I said, looking up from my pile of notes. Saffa crept in and closed the door quietly behind her.

"Why are you creeping about?" I patted the duvet beside me.

Saffa walked over and collapsed on to my bed. Her face crumpling as if she were about to cry. I quickly enveloped her skinny frame in my arms.

"It's alright Saffa, let it all out," I said, cradling her head with my hand, but she didn't cry.

Suddenly, she sat upright and took a deep breath. "It's Baba."

"Oh God, what's he said to you now?"

"He came in my room earlier and sat with me. I thought he'd come in to see if I was okay. Mum already warned me she was going to tell him about my arm and she promised nothing would happen to me."

"What did he do?"

"He didn't do anything, just as she'd promised. It was just what he said. He gave me an hour lecture on self-harm and how Allah will punish me for deliberately hurting myself, and how no one will marry me in the future now that I've disfigured myself."

"Saffa, you know that's not true! Don't listen to him," I took her hands in mine, careful not to go anywhere near her bandage in case I hurt her arm by mistake. "Have you spoken to Kareem? Have you told him about everything that's been going on?"

Saffa shook her head. "I broke up with him."

"You did what? Why?"

"I know Kareem is kind and good. I know he would have taken care of me. I just felt like it was a waste of time. Kareem and I don't have a future. Baba would never let me marry into a secular family like his who drink, don't pray and don't fast in Ramadan." Saffa looked down and started to play with the edges of her bandage. "I felt like I had cried out all my tears and there was no more. I just wanted a release so I took a blade out of one of Baba's razors and tried just a little cut at first. It hurt but it felt good. And then I couldn't stop because I wanted to cry so badly and the tears wouldn't come, so I had to keep cutting."

"Please don't cut anymore. I don't want to lose you," I said, stroking her hair. "Whenever you feel like cutting come and talk to me instead."

"I'll try my best," Saffa replied, and she put her head on my shoulder.

Nawaf

Before university closed for spring break, the students in my programme were invited to a conference organised by the government. One of the panels at the conference was on gender laws in the country, and as someone who was passionate about women's rights, I rushed to get a seat.

The main discussion was whether the gender laws in the country enabled women to excel in society. I put up my hand. The moderator pointed at me and his assistant came over with the microphone.

"There are laws that grant women the right to be educated, the right to work, the right to drive and the right to vote, but why is it that women still must have a letter of no objection from a male guardian before they can actually step into the workplace? It's still a patriarchal society," I said.

My classmates clapped while the panellists and the rest of the audience looked bewildered. The 'patriarchy' was a relatively new word in the Gulf in 2010. No one had even heard of a feminist back then.

"Err, well, due to the sponsorship laws in the country, this is difficult," the government minister on the panel said in English, lost for words.

After the session, I left the banquet hall that was being used for the conference to grab some food from the waiters.

"Excuse me miss!" a man called out in Arabic.

I turned around and saw a very tall, broad-shouldered Gulf man, dressed in a *thowb* and *egaal*, following me. I could tell by looking at him that he was someone important, from the way his *thowb* was buttoned all the way up to the top, to the expensive-looking silver pen that was perched inside his chest pocket, the round silver cufflinks encrusted with black onyx that held his *thowb* sleeves together, and his shiny, black, lace-up leather shoes.

Ordinary Gulf men wore chunky leather sandals called *na'aal*. It was only businessmen and government officials who wore lace-up shoes with their *thowbs*.

"Excuse me, miss, where are you from?" he asked.

"Oh, I'm half English and half Egyptian," I replied.

My eyes were distracted by the trays of sweet delicacies that were floating around the lobby outside the banqueting hall. I wished he would hurry up and finish whatever it was he wanted to say so I could eat before the next panel started.

"I heard your question during the last panel. You speak English so well, like a native English person, but when I look at you, I can see Arab features. I was so confused," he said, laughing.

"Yeah, I get people telling me that all the time. I was born and brought up in London."

"Wow, I go to London a lot for work," he said. "Sorry, let me introduce myself. I'm Nawaf."

"It's lovely to meet you. I'm Sara."

"What do you do?" he asked. "Are you studying? Working?"

"I'm actually in my final year studying Political Science at the state university."

"How funny!" he exclaimed. "You're studying Political Science here in my country, while I studied Political Science in yours!"

I took a good look at him. He was quite handsome. He didn't have a beard or goatee, just a thick moustache, which was unlike most Gulf men. It was usually middle-aged men who sported just a moustache, but this guy couldn't have been older than his early thirties. He was well built and he had a little dimple in his chin.

"I better go back inside, the next panel's going to start and my friends are inside waiting for me," I lied.

"Oh yes, of course," Nawaf said. "I'd love to stay in touch with you. Would you mind if I asked for your number?"

I was a sucker for a bit of charm and good looks, so I gave him my number. I knew I had promised Heba no more Gulf guys, but I hadn't promised myself!

We walked back into the banqueting hall for the next panel. I sat back in my chair but my eyes followed him across the hall. I noticed he sat in the front row, in one of the fancy, deep-red, upholstered chairs with gold frames that were reserved for government ministers, diplomats, members of the royal family and VIPs.

He clearly was important, but who was he? What would someone like him want with someone like me? I wasn't some glamorous TV presenter or actress that I assumed he usually dated. You know the type—long, glossy, black Arabic hair, designer clothes, and a plastic surgeon in Lebanon on speed dial.

I was plain old me. A university student with a big nose, wild curly hair, confusing half-English half-Egyptian features, and boring blouses and long skirts from Marks & Spencer. I still hadn't even figured out what I wanted to do after I graduated, so what was interesting or alluring about me?

To be honest, I didn't focus on the rest of the conference. I just kept looking over to get a glimpse of Nawaf, wondering if he'd also turn around to try to look at me, and our eyes would meet. But he seemed preoccupied. A government minister was sat next to him wearing a thin black cape with gold embroidery called a *bisht*—a garment only worn by Gulf men who were important. He was speaking into Nawaf's ear.

The conference ended at 5pm. One of my female peers tapped me on the shoulder.

"I can't let you wait for a taxi, let me give you a lift," she insisted.

I smiled. "Thanks, that would be great."

As I stood in the lobby, waiting for her to finish going to the toilet, Nawaf came out of the banqueting hall. He was alone and walked straight up to me.

"How are you getting home?" Nawaf asked. "Can I give you a ride?"

"Oh, thank you, but my friend is giving me a lift," I replied.

"I hope we can meet again soon and that I get the chance to know you better," he said. "It would be an honour."

"Thank you," I replied, trying not to blush. "The honour is mine." My ride was coming out of the ladies' bathroom. "I've got to go, but message me."

"I will," Nawaf said, smiling.

Gulf Men... Again

Nawaf texted me that evening.

I just can't get over how beautiful you are in your hijab and your abaya. For so long I've been hoping to meet a woman who combined East with West. The elegance of an Arab woman with the sophistication of a Western woman.

I couldn't believe that this very important man was mesmerised by me!

Now that I was officially on spring break, I'd no longer have opportunities to make or receive phone calls from guys during the day. I sighed as I texted him about Baba. I felt like I was on autopilot as I told him that I had a strict father and that it'd be nearly impossible for me to call him at home. So he texted back his email address and told me to communicate with him on Windows Live Messenger.

Looking back, two of my biggest flaws in my twenties was my impulsiveness and my naivety when it came to men. I wanted to give every man a chance, refusing to generalise all Gulf men based on an ex's bad behaviour.

After only two days of chatting on Windows Live Messenger, Nawaf suggested a lunch date. I didn't play hard to get as I'd been advised to so many times by Heba. I agreed to go out with him straight away.

I'd yet again made it on to the Dean's list that semester so it would buy me favours from Baba, and he wouldn't object to me going out with my 'friends from university.' We set a date for the following Monday.

I felt very self-conscious about going out with Nawaf. I felt like I needed to be the elegant, sophisticated woman that I was convinced he was used to.

The morning of our lunch date, I slid open the door of my wardrobe and looked at my small collection of four *abayas* in frustration. I chose the best *abaya* I owned, the one I kept for special occasions. It was made of a glossy black material and had bat wings. It only had three buttons at the top, so you had to pull it over the top of your head to get it on, like a dress. The sleeves were tight like shirt cuffs and they were studded with fake white pearls. White pearly beads were studded haphazardly over the front and back of the bodice too. It was the best *abaya* I had and the obvious choice.

I put on full party make-up, knowing I'd get away with it as Baba was at work and Mum had no issues with me wearing it. I put on pink lip gloss, not wanting to risk another episode where I wasn't able to remove red lipstick before getting home.

I told Nawaf to pick me up at a small shopping mall that was a short walk from our house. I wasn't having him pick me up anywhere near our house.

As I went out of the front door, Mum called out to me from the living room to be home by *maghrib* prayer.

Once I'd got around the corner, I took the end of my black *shayla*, and I used it as a *ghishwa* to cover my face.

As I left my relatively quiet residential neighbourhood and walked the busy commercial streets, Gulf men slowed down in their cars and stared at me as I walked along the pavement. I suppose with my *ghishwa* on they assumed I was a Gulf woman, and Gulf women didn't walk about in the street and cross roads in the sun at midday. Gulf women were chauffeured around from shop door to shop door.

When I got to the mall, I called Nawaf to let him know I'd arrived.

"Come down to the basement parking," he instructed. "I'm only two minutes away. I'll be in a silver Range Rover."

I took the escalator down to the basement level and waited by the automatic doors, where the air conditioning blew directly into my face, not wanting to wait outside in a hot and stuffy car park.

He was fifteen minutes late.

As I climbed into the car, Nawaf motioned at me with his finger to keep silent. He was talking on the phone to someone through an earpiece. We drove off in the direction of the city centre, and a few minutes later he wrapped up his telephone conversation.

"Sorry about that. I had an important work phone call."

"I thought Gulf men could just come in and out of work as they please?" I asked.

He laughed. "Not where I work."

"Where do you work?"

"If I told you I'd have to kill you," he said, and continued to laugh. There was something about his tone that unnerved me. "Where do you want to go for lunch?"

"Honestly, I'm not picky. I don't mind. Wherever," I replied.

"Ah, you women, you can never make your minds up!" he said, laughing again.

I noticed when he smiled he bared all his teeth, which were slightly yellow around the edges. He'd told me he was thirty, but sitting next to him, I would have put him at thirty-five or thirty-six. He'd said he was divorced and that he wouldn't marry a Gulf woman again because they were spoilt and he wanted a foreign wife next time. I'd never dated anyone who was divorced before but it didn't bother me.

"How about we have lunch at the same hotel we were at for the conference last week?" he suggested. "I know a very elegant Lebanese restaurant there—if you don't mind of course?"

"Yeah, sure, I like Lebanese food," I replied.

I wasn't going to turn down an offer for lunch at a luxury hotel.

There was no one at the Lebanese restaurant, which had an outside terrace that looked on to the hotel's gardens. Heavy red brocade curtains hung over the windows, and the chairs looked like French chalais chairs.

When Nawaf walked in, the restaurant manager called him *sheikh* and immediately started kissing up to him. I couldn't stand it when non-Gulf Arabs who worked in the Gulf did that. I didn't care if you were Gulf or not, I treated everyone the same.

The moment the restaurant manager addressed Nawaf with the word *sheikh* it could only mean one thing—he was definitely from the royal family. There were only three reasons why you would call an Arab man *sheikh*: either they were old (which Nawaf wasn't), a religious leader (again not applicable), or a member of the royal family.

After the restaurant manager had stopped fussing over Nawaf, he led us over to a table in the family section—which was in a corridor in the restaurant restricted to couples and families. The tables were arranged back to back in rows, with wooden lattice dividers between them that offered some privacy.

The manager handed over just one menu to Nawaf and without asking me what I wanted to eat, he ordered a selection of kebabs and chips for the both of us. It always confused me how Gulf men were gentlemanly and courteous towards women in some aspects, but completely indifferent and inconsiderate in others. I know some women may have found that rude but I didn't mind. I wasn't a fussy eater.

Nawaf told me about all the countries he'd visited and I pretended to know about them but truthfully I'd only been to Egypt. I felt like I was in a scene from *Pretty Woman*.

"Have you ever been camping?" Nawaf asked as the waiter cleared away our plates and brought him a pot of steaming Moroccan mint tea in a traditional Arabian teapot.

"Well, I once did a weekend of activities in the English countryside. We slept in barracks with a Muslim Girls Scouts group before I moved out here." I took the small round teacup he offered me.

"No, I mean real camping. You know, desert style, like the Bedouins," he said.

I shook my head.

Nawaf smiled. "I should take you to my family's camp

next week when I'm back from my work trip to London. The camping season is about to finish and our manservants will disassemble the tents soon."

"Well, I could go for the day, but there's no way I can spend the night," I said.

Most of my Gulf girlfriends' families had their own campsites in the desert, which they spent every weekend at during the winter season, and I'd always wanted to go.

Overall it was a pretty good date. When I got home, I took the cordless phone up to my bedroom. I dialled Heba's number and told her about Nawaf, speaking in a hushed tone to prevent my family from eavesdropping.

"I thought we agreed no more Gulf guys!" she exclaimed. "They mess you about every time and then you come back to me crying."

"Nawaf isn't some little boy like Fahad, he's a mature man. I'm sure he's serious about me."

"Listen," Heba said in a softer tone. "I love you and don't want you to get hurt. These guys date us, but they don't marry us. And you're the type that wants to get married, not just date."

Heba didn't care that I was going to the desert with a guy. Her issue was that he was a Gulf guy.

"Are you forgetting that it was you who pushed me into going out with Aziz, who was a Gulfie too?" I challenged her.

Heba went silent.

"Just be careful, Sara," Heba said.

"It'll be fine," I said defiantly.

Once we hung up, I texted Nawaf to tell him I was free the following week to go on a day trip to the desert with him.

"Another Gulf guy?" Sophie asked.

I laughed. "I was just so determined to get one, despite the warnings."

"Nawaf seems pretty nice."

I looked down at my lukewarm cup of tea. "He did, didn't he?"

Sand Dunes

"You're asking me to go out all the time now *ya Sara* and I don't like it. Spend some time at home. Learn how to cook. Be useful," Baba said after I asked him if I could go out on Monday for the whole day. "And every time with Heba. Why can't you make friends with the *amus'* daughters?"

"I don't have anything in common with them," I replied quietly, not wanting to say the truth.

The one time I'd been forced into an Eid gathering with his friends' wives and daughters, I was bored out of my brain. I knew if I told Baba that it would piss him off and then he'd say no.

"It's the last week before the new semester starts, and it's my final semester Baba. After this week I won't be able to go out as much anyway with all my final essays and exams coming up."

He went quiet and picked up his book on Islamic law. "Fine, go."

Since I'd broken up with Fahad, who used to supply me with phone credit, I had to be a lot more careful about how many text messages I sent. I didn't want to spend all my monthly allowance on credit for Heba's mobile phone.

ME: *I can spend the whole day with you on Monday!!!*

NAWAF: *Excellent news! I'll pick you up from that same mall at 10am.*

I won't lie. I was nervous about travelling so far with a guy. On Sunday, I spent most of the day sat on the sofa watching TV, but not actually focusing on it. Should I go? Or should I cancel?

I tried to suppress my anxiety. I told myself it would be a fun day out and that I should take this opportunity. I may not get the chance to go camping in the desert again.

*

Nawaf was dressed in Western clothes when he came to pick me up from the local mall. He was wearing off-white linen shorts and a baby blue T-shirt that said California Dreamin' with a picture of a sunset printed on the front; the type of T-shirt you see in American road trip movies.

Out of his *thowb* he looked even taller and broader. I didn't feel like I was dressed in the right clothes for an outdoor adventure. I was wearing long, wide black trousers under my *abaya* and a short-sleeved tunic which had a geometric blue, black and white print. The fabric of the tunic was slightly sheer and it had a low plunging neckline. It was perhaps one of the most revealing items I had in my wardrobe, but with my *abaya* over the top, no one would have ever known. I was wearing the same bat-wing *abaya* with fake pearl beads that I'd worn for lunch with Nawaf the week before.

He'd brought a gold Lexus four-wheeler this time instead of his sporty Range Rover. It took almost two hours to reach the campsite. I was excited imagining Bedouin-style tents, the ones that were made from that heavy black fabric with horizontal beige stripes, and those red and black patterned floor cushions, like the ones Fahad had in his *majlis*.

Before we got to the sandy part, where the desert began, we had to stop at a petrol station, where a couple of Indian labourers dressed in orange boiler suits let air out of Nawaf's car tyres so he could ride over the sand. I, of course, had my *ghishwa* on, and they paid no attention to me.

Once the tyres were ready and Nawaf had pressed a few notes of money into the men's hands through his open window, we set off into the desert. The car bumped up and down. The wooden *tasbeeh* beads he'd hung around the front-view mirror kept hitting the windscreen every time we went over a bump.

I looked at the barren landscape around me as the Saudi Arabian singer Rashed Al-Majed serenaded us from the car's loudspeakers. We passed towering sand dunes on the way.

I saw a group of quad bikes racing up and down the dunes. The young Gulf men who were riding them had their *thowbs* hoisted up to their waists, dark sunglasses on and *ghutras* wrapped around their faces like face veils.

Half an hour later I saw a group of tents ahead of us, enclosed by a tall wire fence.

An Indian man sat on a white plastic chair at the gated entrance of the campsite. When we approached he immediately stood up and said, "*Salam alaik ya sheikh,*" Arabic for "Peace be upon you oh sheikh," before unlocking the gate and opening it so that Nawaf could drive inside.

"Are Saddam and Fairous here?" Nawaf asked him.

"Yes sir, they're already in the kitchen preparing lunch," the gatekeeper replied.

The kitchen?

It turned out that these weren't the old-school Bedouin tents I'd imagined. From the outside they looked ordinary enough. They were huge, rectangular, beige tents with flaps that worked as doors, with strings you tied through metal holes in order to close them. There were five of them arranged in a semi-circle, and then a small raised cabin with steps, which was a short distance away from the tents was a bathroom.

The tent on the far right was the kitchen and the largest tent, which was next to the kitchen, was the living room. Two medium-sized tents to the left of the living room were bedrooms and the fifth tent, on the far left and slightly removed from the others, was where the manservants slept.

We got out of the car and I followed Nawaf towards the main tent. He took his trainers off just outside the tent's entrance and left them on a little rug of artificial green grass, and I did the same with my ballerina flats. He untied the strings on the metal loopholes, lifted up the heavy beige flap and allowed me to go inside first before following in after me and tying the strings shut.

Instead of the typical black and red floor cushions and red rugs, a staple in most Gulf tents and *majlises*, this tent was elegantly set out with champagne-coloured floor sofas set in wooden frames and arranged in an L shape along the back and left sides of the tent. Off-white cushions and armrests were propped up along the sofas. Several glass coffee tables were positioned in front of the sofas, laden with silver bowls containing expensive, wrapped chocolates and an assortment of nuts and fruit.

To the right of the tent was a massive flat-screen TV and three different games consoles. Several Moroccan pouffes were laid out in a semi-circle in front of the TV. Two big, plush, beige rugs covered the entire length of the sandy floor.

"What do you think?" he asked.

"It's lovely. I wish my family had this. Do you use it much?"

"My brothers come here with their friends during the weeknights and the women come with the kids and stay here on the weekends," Nawaf explained, sitting down on to one of the Moroccan pouffes and switching on the big portable air-conditioning unit with a remote control. He switched on the TV and put on a music channel. Mohammed Abdu was singing.

I took off my black *shayla* and let it rest on my shoulders, but kept my *abaya* on. Nawaf noticed.

"You don't need to wear your *abaya* in here. No one will come in unless I call them," Nawaf said. "Take it off."

"I'm good," I replied.

"It's up to you," he said, shrugging. He stood up and walked to the flap at the entrance of the tent, and untied the strings again. "Put your *shayla* and shoes back on. Let's take the car for a ride on the dunes before lunch."

Back in his car, we set off towards the sand dunes. As we approached the bottom of the first dune he stopped, turned to me and asked, "Are you ready?" before he shifted the car gear, pushed his foot down hard on the gas pedal and we sped up to the top of the dune.

I was terrified that we would roll backwards or topple off the top of the dune and the car would flip over. As we reached the top of the dune, I felt like I was on a rollercoaster, when you can see the sharp drop below you. Nawaf knew what he was doing because we sped smoothly down the dune and back onto the flat sandy area. I gripped the handle at the top of the passenger side window with both hands.

"Are you ready for the next one?" he asked.

I just wanted to get back to the tent in one piece. I nodded.

We went up the next dune, which was even higher than that last one, but thankfully not as steep. However, mid-way down, the car got stuck in the sand. Nawaf pushed and pushed on the gas pedal, but all we could hear were the car wheels turning furiously in the sand, the car not moving an inch.

He sighed and got out of the car to take a look.

"There's too much sand under the back wheels," he shouted to me, "I'm going to need help."

"Am I going to have to stay here on my own?" I asked.

"I won't be long. Just keep the doors locked. There are lots of young men, around, one of them will be able to help," he said, and off he went.

Well, this date was turning out great.

I didn't have to wait long. A black Land Cruiser approached, with Nawaf in the passenger seat, and another Gulf guy driving.

The man parked his car in front on a flatter patch of sand. I took the end of my *shayla* and covered my face.

The man opened the boot of the car and took out a huge piece of heavy-duty fabric cable, tying one end to the bottom of the back of his Land Cruiser and the other end to the bottom of the front of Nawaf's four-wheeler. They exchanged some words and Nawaf got back into the car with me.

"See, I told you I would find one of the *shabaab* to help." He grinned.

The man got into his car, stuck his arm out of the car window and signalled at Nawaf to get ready. Nawaf switched on the engine, and again the car wheels turned furiously in their place. Slowly we were being pulled out of the sand and down towards the flat area.

Nawaf descended from the car, untied the cable and gave it back to the man, and they shook hands.

"I think that's enough excitement for today," Nawaf said, when he got back into the car. "Let's get some food."

The Middle Of Nowhere

"Come, we're having something special for lunch," Nawaf said, and he led me by the hand to the far end of the campsite. His manservants Saddam and Fairaus were stood over a burning pit in the sand.

I was surprised that he was holding my hand in front of them. Saddam and Fairaus dug away the sand with their bare hands, and out of it emerged a huge steel cooking pot, which needed the both of them to lift it out of the sand together. The gatekeeper was stood to the side, grilling fish on a barbecue.

"They caught these fish this morning from the sea," Nawaf told me proudly.

I smiled and pretended to be impressed. I hated eating whole fish. It wasn't the fish that I disliked, but the tedious task of feeling for bones while eating it and the fear of choking on a bone by mistake.

One of the manservants opened the lid of the pot, and a stream of steam rushed out, revealing lamb *kabsa*.

"This is a special way of cooking food, on a coal fire covered with sand," Nawaf explained.

I found the idea of the sand oven pretty cool, but the meat *kabsa* was nothing new. I wondered if Gulfies ate anything other than rice and meat. I had to hand it to the Egyptians, they had a wider variety of traditional dishes.

Back in London, before he'd ceased all forms of domestic activity, Baba had taught Mum how to cook all sorts of delicious Egyptian meals. Vegetables stuffed with rice called *mahshi*, a pastry pie filled with minced beef and fried onions called *goulash* and a mixture of rice, macaroni, lentils and crispy brown onions called *koshari* were my favourite Egyptian dishes.

Saddam and Fairaus carried the giant steel pot into the kitchen tent and Nawaf led me back to the living room tent.

Saddam stood outside the tent and said in broken Arabic, "Baba, can I come in?"

Servants called their employers Mum and Dad in Arabic as a sign of respect, but I found it derogatory.

"Come in Saddam," Nawaf replied.

Saddam was dressed in a black T-shirt and a white and blue chequered cloth which was wrapped around his legs and tied at his hips called an *izar*. He came inside and laid some plastic sheeting on the floor.

"You know my father only hired him because his name is Saddam!" Nawaf laughed.

I looked at Nawaf, flabbergasted, and he stopped laughing immediately.

"Shall we bring the food in now Baba?" Saddam asked.

"Yes, yes, bring it," Nawaf replied impatiently, waving his hand as if to hurry Saddam along.

Nawaf's arrogant attitude was starting to get on my nerves. I knew this was how a lot of Gulfies behaved towards South

Asians. They were brought up to be dismissive of them by their parents. I kept quiet, not wanting to piss Nawaf off.

Saddam and Fairaus carefully carried in a huge, round tray of lamb *kabsa*, followed by another tray of barbecued fish.

"Are other people joining us for lunch?" I asked, slightly worried that he might have invited other people to the tent without telling me.

"No, it's just me and you," he replied casually.

I knew I could eat an impressive amount of food, but this was enough food to feed at least twenty people!

"What are you going to do with what we don't eat?" I asked.

"The servants will eat it and they'll get manservants from other camps to join them."

I noticed that despite the fact he wasn't as familiar with English and Western pop culture as Fahad was, Nawaf was more refined. He ate his rice with a spoon and not his fingers. He took a couple of pieces of barbecued fish off the tray and put them on my plate.

"You didn't try any of the fish yet. I had them caught especially for you."

I really didn't want to eat the two fish that I felt were staring at me from my plate with their googly eyes, but I also didn't want to offend Nawaf.

"Are you scared of the bones?" Nawaf laughed and I felt like a child. "Here, let me help you." He ripped off little pieces of fish from the bone. "Would you like me to feed it to you?" He held a piece near my face.

I knew he was trying to be funny but I found his attitude patronising. I laughed nervously and took the piece of fish from his fingers and popped it into my mouth.

After we had eaten, Nawaf shouted, "Saddam! Saddam!" and Saddam and Fairaus hurried into the tent and removed the trays.

Once they'd finished clearing everything away, Nawaf closed the flap of the tent, looping the strings through the metal holes and tying tight knots.

"I feel like I need a nap after that lunch," he said, stretching his arms wide open. He took off his California Dreamin' T-shirt, revealing his bare chest, and sat on the floor beside me.

"Err. . . oh. . . okay," I said, sneaking a glance at him.

He was fit. He had a strip of black hair on his toned chest. He gave a floor cushion a few hard smacks before he sat on it. I sat awkwardly beside him, watching the music channel, which had now switched to Latin pop. Shakira shook her hips on the TV screen.

"Come and lie down beside me," he said with his arm outstretched towards me, motioning to me to come and lie in the crook of his arm.

Something in his voice was so commanding that I did as he said.

"Put your head on my chest," he said, pulling me towards him. "Can you feel my heart?" He grabbed my hand and held it on top of his chest. "It's beating fast because I like you."

"Oh, okay." I seemed to have lost the ability to say full sentences.

"Why are you still wearing that thing?" he asked, pulling at the sleeve of my *abaya*. "Come on, get comfortable."

I reluctantly took it off and immediately felt exposed. I looked down and remembered I was wearing the sheer printed tunic, the one with the deep V-neckline. Stupid choice.

He suddenly sat up, and I saw his eyes move up and down my body greedily.

"Your body is so. . . sexy," he said. His gaze fixed on my breasts.

I blushed under his gaze. I may not have been head over heels for Nawaf, but I'd longed for physical affection from a man ever since I'd been with Fahad.

Nawaf reached over, took my right hand, held it up to his lips, which were dark from smoking, and kissed the back of it softly. He took my other hand in his and pulled me towards him. I sat awkwardly in his lap, and he wrapped his arms around my waist and pulled me closer to him, so that my breasts were pressed up against his chest.

He pushed his lips on mine and I smelt the faint scent of cigarettes. The sharp bristles of his moustache tickled the top of my upper lip. I stroked his face with both my hands, the stubble on his cheeks feeling rough against my fingers.

He removed the tortoiseshell clip from my blow-dried and straightened hair, allowing it to fall down my back, and ran his hands through it as he kissed my lips. Then he pressed his hands against my small boobs and bit my cheeks and lips.

"That hurts!" I exclaimed.

Ignoring me, he stuck his tongue in my left ear, and it felt really wet and slimy. I was starting to feel hot, even though the air-conditioning unit was right beside us. He was becoming a little rough and overexcited, tugging at my hair and biting down on my bottom lip hard, all while gyrating underneath me.

"Come here you *gahba*, you slut," he said, and he grabbed at the metal clasp that closed my black trousers at the waist.

"No, no, no!" I cried out, trying to hold the two parts of my trousers together.

"You've made me horny," Nawaf said, and pushed me on to my back aggressively so that my head hit the rug beneath me.

He pulled off my trousers even though I kicked my legs, trying to get him away from me. What did he think he was doing?

"Give me back my trousers!" I shouted.

He glared at me. "Why don't you shut up?" He threw my black trousers out of my reach.

I tried to stand up but he grabbed me by the neck and pushed me down on to my face. I started to cry. The volume of the music on the TV grew louder. *I Know You Want Me* by Pitbull echoed around the tent.

It was impossible to break free. He lay on top of my back and he was so heavy that I felt like I was being crushed. He pushed into me and the pain. The pain was indescribable. It felt like I was being stabbed and ripped apart.

"Please," I sobbed hysterically. "Please just stop. It hurts. Just take me home. I swear I won't tell anyone if you just stop and take me home."

"I told you to shut up!" he yelled. "You asked for this."

We were in a camp in the middle of nowhere. No one would rush to my rescue. I was sure his manservants could hear me but they were probably terrified of Nawaf and would not come to my rescue. God knows if they tried to save me he might murder all of us.

I tried to turn my face, hoping if he saw my pain that he would have an ounce of feeling and stop, but he just pushed my neck down again. I ceased trying and told myself just to shut up. Maybe if I was still and stopped fighting it would end quicker. I grasped on to the woollen tassels of the beige carpet and closed my eyes tight, as the pain seared through me.

Nawaf suddenly exclaimed, "I'm going to come!"

A second later I felt something wet on my back.

"Stay there, don't move," he ordered, but he had stopped shouting. I felt him wipe my back with what must have been a wad of tissues.

I slowly pushed myself up on to my knees and it took all the strength in the world to stand up. My legs felt heavy and numb. He pulled another wad of tissues out of a tissue box, walked over and gently wiped my legs and thighs.

"Go to the bathroom and clean yourself up," he said softly.

I quickly pulled my *abaya* over my half-naked body. He untied the strings on the metal loopholes and lifted up the flap of the tent so I could go outside. There was no sign of Saddam and Fairaus. The gatekeeper was sitting on the chair outside the gate completely oblivious.

I put on my ballerina flats and walked slowly behind the tent, where the small bathroom cabin stood, crying with each step. Was I ever going to see my family again? Or would I become one of those girls that I'd heard stories about whose bodies were found discarded in the desert?

Everything felt like it was burning. I had to climb up three steps to get to the door of the bathroom cabin, and held on to either side of the railing as I hoisted myself up each step slowly. I opened the door and inside was a fully decked-out bathroom: toilet, bidet, sink and shower.

I pulled my *abaya* and tunic up to my chest, stood in the shower and turned on the cold water. I washed the blood that had dried on the inside of my thighs and legs. The water turned crimson as it went down the drain. There wasn't enough water in that desert to make me feel clean.

I stepped out of the shower on to the tiled floor. I ripped off a scarf-length amount of toilet paper, rolled it up and dabbed myself dry. Then I washed my hands in the little sink with the oud-scented hand wash before getting dressed.

When I returned to the main tent, Nawaf was sitting on the floor, with his back against a floor cushion. He had his clothes back on and a lit cigarette in one hand.

"Are you still bleeding?" he asked gently.

"Yes," I replied sniffling. I had managed to stop crying.

I took a wad of tissues from the tissue box and lined my knickers with them as I put my trousers back on under my *abaya*. He patted the floor beside me as he placed the cigarette in his mouth for a final drag. Terrified to disobey him I went over and sat next to him.

Nawaf hugged me and held me to his chest. He kissed the top of my head.

"I didn't know you were a virgin," he said. "If I'd known I never would have done it. Now I feel bad."

I thought I was going to throw up.

"I did it because I like you. I'm your boyfriend now, and when I come back from my next trip to London I'm going to bring you back so many gifts."

This man was a psycho.

"My parents are expecting me back home by *maghrib*," I told him quietly.

"Oh, of course," Nawaf said. "I'll get the car ready. Come out in five minutes."

I tried to act as normally as possible, even though my hands were shaking as I wrapped my *shayla* around my hair and picked up my handbag. As Nawaf started up the engine, I put on my shoes and made my way over to the car.

The ride back home was silent. We had to stop again at the same petrol station on the edge of the desert to refill Nawaf's car tyres with air. Mohammed Abdu was playing again on the radio. This time it was the song *Al-Amaaken* which means 'The Places.'

"Al amaan, ween al amaan?" Mohammed Abdu sang, which means, "Security, where is security?" The lyrics about safety and security reverberated deep within me as we travelled along the desert highway in silence. The sky to our left was a beautiful mix of blue, pink and gold as the sun began to set.

My chest felt tight and I quickly had a drink of water. "Can I take five minutes?"

"Of course," Sophie said pausing her recording. I stood up and went outside the small café we had stumbled upon a few days ago. We felt the Caffè Nero staff were getting annoyed with us buying one drink every two hours.

I took a deep breath of the cool air and sighed. I hated how Nawaf still affected me till this day. I glanced at my phone. It was 5pm. We were wrapping up in an hour.

"You're going to be okay. You're strong," I said to myself. I took another deep breath before going back inside.

Secrets

As we approached the city Nawaf said, "Don't tell anyone what happened or who I am."

"I won't," I said quietly.

"Don't make me have to put our Intelligence on you," he said, laughing but I knew he wasn't joking.

"You can trust me. Everyone trusts me with secrets."

I had no intention of telling anyone at home, or Heba either. Baba would kill me, Mum would probably have a nervous breakdown, and Heba would kill Nawaf!

"I'll be back from London in three weeks," he said as he dropped me off back at the local mall.

He then did something that I'm ashamed of to this day. He pressed the equivalent of £100 into my hand. I refused to take it and tried to give it back.

"Keep it, you might need something," he said. "Don't forget that I'm going to bring you back beautiful gifts from London."

I was too scared to try and give it back a second time, so I put it into my handbag quickly and got out of the car. I felt like a prostitute. To him my virginity was worth £100 and some gifts from London.

I checked the time on my secret phone. It had just gone past the call to *maghrib* prayer. Baba would be back home soon, and Mum would be expecting me to be home in time for dinner. I paced around the mall in a circle several times, knowing I needed to go home, but scared that Mum or Baba would see that something was up.

I went to the ladies' bathroom and saw that my eyes were still red and puffy from all the crying. I felt like I needed to talk to someone, to say what had happened to me, but I didn't know who.

I made my way out of the mall. With every step I took it stung me down below and the wad of tissues in my knickers felt uncomfortable.

When I finally reached home, I was so sure that Mum and Baba would take one look at my face and know. Baba was sitting at the head of the dinner table, waiting for his dinner to be served as usual, and Mum was laying out the placemats.

"Are you eating with us?" Mum asked as I walked past the dining room.

"No I'm full," I said.

I took a plastic bag and the jar of table salt from the kitchen, went upstairs to the bathroom, and locked myself inside. I sat and waited on top of the cold toilet lid for the bathtub to fill up, and emptied out half the jar of salt into the bathwater. I pulled my *shayla* and *abaya* off and peeled off my tunic and trousers. I unclipped my bra and rolled down my knickers. The tissues were soaked with blood and it had seeped through to my knickers. I checked my trousers for bloodstains, but there weren't any.

I put the knickers into the plastic bag and double knotted it. I'd have to take it outside to the rubbish skip myself, because I didn't want anyone discovering it in the bin. The blood was a pinkish red.

I carefully climbed into the bathtub and lowered myself in gently, wincing as the salty water hit me. It stung for the first several minutes, but after that it started to settle down.

As I sat in the hot bathwater, the events of the previous eight hours did a playback. I cried silently, my tears added to the depth of the bathwater as I realised what I'd just got myself into. I didn't move even when the water had gone cold. I jumped from the loud knocking on the door.

"You've been in there for ages!" Mum's voice said through the door. "Are you alive?"

"I'm coming out in a bit," I replied, and pulled out the bathplug.

There in the bathroom, water dripping off my body, I texted Nawaf.

Please delete my number and never contact me ever again.

He replied immediately.

If you're sure that's what you want I won't.

And he never did.

The next morning, it suddenly occurred to me that my last semester at university was beginning in a week's time, and that I'd have to hold myself together until I graduated. I promised myself that under no circumstances was I going to break down in front of my family and let slip what had happened. I knew that if Baba found out, I'd lose my university degree literally months away from graduating. I needed that university degree so I could make a life for myself.

Now that I was no longer a virgin, I could say goodbye to getting married to a Gulfie, or even an Arab. No one would marry a non-virgin who wasn't divorced or widowed. I was now spoiled goods. I was going to focus on getting a good-paying job and becoming financially independent so I could finally escape Baba and his dictatorship at home.

I tried my best to shut out any memories or flashbacks and channelled everything into graduating from university. My university textbooks became my life, something which made Baba happy, as I stopped asking him to go out with my friends or attend 'weddings.'

Six days later, it was the first day of my final semester, and I still hadn't stopped bleeding. I also noticed little flesh like lumps when I wiped myself after using the toilet.

I started to really get worried, and decided to pay a visit to the female doctor at the campus medical clinic. She was a kind Iraqi doctor who I'd been to many times throughout my four years at university.

"It's part of my job to keep what you tell me in confidence. I will not judge you," the doctor reassured me.

I told her what happened in the desert and that I'd been bleeding for six days.

"Can you check my hymen? Have I been fully broken in? What if I'm pregnant?" I asked her, talking quickly.

"I'm sorry this happened to you and believe it or not, you're not the first girl who has come to me telling me the same thing about other men. Ask Allah for forgiveness. If you didn't have bad intentions Allah will forgive you. If this man didn't ejaculate inside you it's almost impossible that you're pregnant, so don't worry. I'm afraid I cannot give you a physical examination unless I inform the police; this is the law in this country."

"I don't want to tell the police," I said, panicking.

"It's your choice," the doctor said. "I can prescribe you some antiseptic cream to apply on the area two to three times a day for ten days and a cream that will help the wound heal. It sounds like he may have torn some small blood vessels."

I took the handwritten prescription she gave me and she smiled at me kindly as I thanked her and left her office. I handed in my prescription at the pharmacy counter and was given two creams before I made my way across the campus for my first lecture. I had never felt so alone.

Sophie switched off her audio recorder and sat back in her chair. I could see she the tears in her eyes.

"Sara, I had no idea. You've never spoken about it in your articles or on social media."

I took her hand in mine. We'd been meeting up every day over the past week and it almost felt as if we were friends. I supposed that was natural when you were sharing the innermost details of your life with someone.

"It's okay, you don't need to say sorry. It's been nine years since it happened. I've decided now is the right time to talk about it, to let the world know what happens when you're raped in an Arab country. It wouldn't have been safe for me to tweet about it while I still lived in the Gulf. Here in London I have freedom of speech again. You don't know how precious that is."

"You're so brave. I don't think I'd have been as brave as you. We'll be changing all names in the documentary, so you're safe," Sophie said, patting the top of my hand. "Shall we wrap up for today? Let's go get a pizza. It's on me. I think we deserve one."

"I can't say no to pizza!" I chuckled.

Invisible

My final semester at university passed by in a blur of essays, pop quizzes and exams. I'd stopped wearing make-up and instead of wearing my *shayla* halfway across my head with my flat-ironed fringe sticking out, I brought the hemline of the front of my *shayla* forward across the top of my forehead, framing it around my face and wrapping it tightly around my head.

Baba thought I'd suddenly become religious and was a lot nicer to me. He'd even started calling me, "Su Su" again, his pet name for me as a child. But the truth was that I felt I was partly to blame for what happened with Nawaf and by disguising myself as a 'religious' woman I hoped it'd put guys off from approaching me.

I decided to combat my guilt and rid myself of my *sharmootah* ways by staying as far away as I could from men. I wanted to be invisible. I was going to dress like a good Muslim woman—bare-faced, hair completely covered, and in my most plain and shapeless *abayas*.

"Are you okay?" Heba asked as we walked to our next lecture together. "You've been acting strange lately."

"Acting strange?" I asked. I thought I'd been doing pretty well at carrying on as if nothing had changed.

"You've been really quiet the past few weeks. I haven't heard you complain about your dad and you haven't gossiped with me once about guys. You're wearing your *shayla* differently. You're not wearing make-up. I'm your best friend, I know when something's going on."

"I'm just stressed about getting good grades so that I graduate with a first-class degree. I mean it is our final semester."

"Hmm," Heba replied. She didn't look satisfied with my answer. "Well, if something's up you know you can tell me."

She didn't have to tell me this. I confided more in Heba than I did in my own mother and sister. I felt I couldn't tell Mum or Saffa everything because I knew Baba was capable of forcing out confessions if he thought I was up to something.

But I just couldn't bring myself to tell Heba about the rape when I'd promised her that I wouldn't go out with a Gulf guy again. I knew she'd try to get involved and use her wide circle of guy friends to find him and beat him up, and getting into a brawl with a member of the royal family was a very bad idea. If he didn't get revenge by murdering them he'd have them put in prison. I wouldn't drag Heba or her friends into this and put their lives in danger.

The worst thing was the flashbacks. Sometimes I'd feel physically sick. I tried really hard not to allow myself to dwell on those thoughts and tried to focus on university.

I was in the toilet in the corridor-like building that housed the Political Science department when I overhead a conversation between Jawhara, Moza and Layla, three Gulf women in my programme. They were applying lip gloss in the mirror and re-arranging their *shaylas*. Then I heard his name. His full name. They were talking about Nawaf and his wife and daughter. I felt as if I was going to vomit and rushed back into the cubicle I'd just come out of, and stood over the toilet bowel, dry retching.

I heard a knock on the cubicle door.

"Are you okay in there?" Moza called.

"I'm fine. *La tahateen*—it's nothing for you to worry about."

Nawaf was married and he had a daughter. Could this get any worse?

*

Carrying my secret was becoming a heavy burden. There were occasions when it'd just be me and Mum in the kitchen and I'd feel the urge to tell her but I'd stop myself. If for any reason it got back to Baba that I'd been out with a man to the middle of the desert and was raped, he wouldn't blame Nawaf, he'd blame me. He'd say it was my fault for going out with a man who wasn't my husband in the first place.

What would happen if he found out? No doubt I'd get the worst beating of my life. Would Baba go as far as killing me? How would he do it? Strangle me to death? No, I had to keep my mouth shut.

"You alright Sara, you seem to be off with the fairies again?" Mum asked, waking me up from my nightmarish daydream.

"Yeah, yeah, I'm fine, just thinking about all the studying I have to do this evening," I replied, and tried to crack a smile.

She gave me a funny look but didn't question me further.

Haram

For the first time in years my relationship with Baba resembled something similar to how it was in London. He'd ask me how my day had been and try to make conversation. He'd only talk with me about Islam, politics and my studies, but it was something. And it killed me inside because I knew he was only being nice to me because I wasn't asking him to go out. He thought I'd become religious. It just proved that his love for me was conditional.

While on the surface of things I'd become 'better behaved,' Saffa was even more rebellious than I'd been at sixteen. She wasn't allowed to go out with her friends outside of school nor was she allowed a mobile phone, so nothing had changed there, but in return for her lack of freedom, she made sure she gave Baba a hard time when he was at home.

I woke up on a Saturday to hear Saffa vomiting. I shoved my duvet to the side, rolled out of bed and walked over to our shared bathroom. The door was ajar.

"You alright, Saffa?" I asked, blinking away the sleep from my eyes.

Saffa stood up, her legs wobbling.

"What've you done to your lip?"

There was a ring in her bottom lip.

"Pierced it myself," she said proudly. "Sterilised a needle and poked it right through. Got the instructions off YouTube. Hurt so much it made me vomit."

"Baba's gonna kill you!"

"No he isn't. He won't do a thing to me."

"Saffa, what have you done?" Mum cried, walking into the bathroom, pushing me aside.

"Haha, you look really cool!" Ahmed said, amused, standing in the bathroom doorway.

Abdullah pushed Ahmed out of the way. "You look like a *sharmootah*."

"Abdullah, you do not say this to your sister," Mum said crossly. "Come on, everyone out of the bathroom, now!"

As soon as Baba came back from one of the *amus'* houses that afternoon and saw Saffa sitting brazenly in the living room watching TV his face dropped.

"What have you done to yourself now?" he shouted, slamming his car keys down on the table.

Ahmed, Abdullah and I sat in deathly silence. Ahmed and I looked at each other with dreaded anticipation.

"I pierced my lip. It's my face, not yours," Saffa replied calmly.

"It's *haram*, Saffa, do you understand the meaning of *haram*? Only ear piercings and nose piercings are allowed in Islam. Take it out now!"

"Everything is *haram*. I'm sick of it. I'm keeping my lip piercing."

"If you never want to get married then keep it. No respectable Arab man will marry you with the way you look. You look disfigured."

Saffa looked at him, her eyes blazing. "I'd never want to marry an Arab man and be unhappy like you and Mum!"

Baba walked over to her and held his hand out to hit her. Ahmed jumped to his feet and put his arm around Baba.

"Leave her alone, Baba, please," Ahmed said calmly. I'd never seen Ahmed react so maturely. Baba put his hand down.

"*Awlaad shayateen*," Baba said, disgusted, and stormed upstairs. He'd just called us the 'children of devils' in Arabic.

"Baba will never be happy with us because of you and Sara," Abdullah said angrily. "You girls cause all the problems in this family."

I rolled my eyes at him. "Alright, Daddy's boy. It's alright for you. Baba lets you do whatever you want because you're a boy."

"He lets me do what I want because I obey his wishes," Abdullah replied self-righteously.

"You watch how Baba changes towards you the minute you step one toe out of line," I said.

"That'll never happen," Abdullah replied.

*

I held myself together until my last day at university. I finished my statistics exam and went home, proud of myself for getting through that final semester.

As I walked through the front door, I heard the sound of the hairdryer coming from upstairs. I followed the sound to find Mum in her bedroom. As she blow-dried her wavy blonde hair, now thinner with age, I sat on the edge of her bed and watched her. At that moment, I felt a strong urge to tell her what had happened to me that day with Nawaf. It was becoming too much to keep to myself. I felt as if I was about to burst.

When she put down her hairdryer and brush, I took a deep breath.

"Mum, there's something I need to tell you, and you have to promise me you won't tell Baba, because he will actually kill me if he finds out."

Mum walked to her bedroom door, closed it firmly and then locked it. She walked back to the dressing table stool and sat back down, facing me.

"Oh God, what now? Go on, tell me."

My hands trembled and my chest felt tight. "Back when it was spring break, I went out with a guy from the royal family. And I. . . he. . .he raped me."

I burst into tears.

"I knew something bad had happened. You've not been yourself for months." Mum started to cry. "How? How did this happen?"

"It was the day I said I was going to be with Heba."

"You lied? How can I keep defending you to Baba when you keep lying to me?"

"How else am I supposed to find my perfect guy and get married? I have to lie."

"First Saffa was attacked and now you've been raped."

"We didn't ask for this," I snapped.

"I know, I know." Mum rubbed her face. "Oh, what will your father say?"

"You can't tell him Mum! Do you know what he'll do to me?"

"I'm sorry," Mum said, pulling me towards her. "I just panicked." She held my face in her hands. "This is not your fault, Sara. Do you hear me? I can't even believe what you girls have been through. This is my fault." Mum put her head in her heads. "I should have lied and taken you and Saffa back months ago, away from this awful place."

I wished she had too.

Breathe

"Saffa, Sara, stay in your bedrooms this evening. Lock your doors," Mum told Saffa and I as the prayer call to *maghrib* went out over the neighbourhood loudspeakers. We knew Baba would pray *maghrib* on his way home from work and be home shortly after that.

"Why? What's going on?" Saffa asked, alarmed.

"I'm going to lie and tell him that Gran is dying so I can go home and take you and Sara with me for good."

"And what about the boys?" Saffa asked. "You can't leave them here."

"No women's refuge will take in two teenage boys. Don't worry. I've got a plan. They'll join us later," Mum said confidently.

My heart was beating with a mixture of excitement and dread. Mum had finally found the courage to do it. Was Baba going to believe her and agree?

The shouting soon started from my parents' bedroom, Ahmed, Saffa and I eavesdropped from the safety of the corridor.

"You're lying! I know you're lying!" Baba shouted. "You're trying to run away! Do you think I'm stupid?"

"My mother is dying, Mustafa! Stop being so crazy. Are you going to deny me the chance to tell my mother goodbye? Despite everything that's happened, she's my mother."

"You're lying, and if you don't tell me the real reason I'll put a travel ban on everyone in this household!"

"Alright, do you want to know the real reason, Mustafa? Do you? I'm saving your daughters from this hellhole. One daughter was sexually assaulted and the other one was raped. This country has destroyed them."

Ahmed turned pale and looked at me. "Lock yourself in your bedroom. Now!"

I ran to my room and locked the door behind me, my heart pounding wildly. I used all my strength to push my bed against the bedroom door.

"If I see her I don't know what I'll do to her!" Baba screamed. "I told you we should have had her circumcised when she was a baby!"

It wasn't until many years later that Mum told me that she had to physically stop him from leaving the bedroom that evening because he wanted to beat me. He stayed in their bedroom for the rest of that evening.

As a punishment for being raped, Baba wouldn't allow me to go to my graduation ceremony. I had worked so hard and I couldn't experience wearing a graduation robe, holding my degree certificate rolled up and tied with a ribbon.

On the morning of my graduation ceremony, I texted Heba and told her I couldn't make it. I lied and said I was too ill. She replied back instantly.

Oh man, Sara, on our graduation day? I'm so sorry. We'll celebrate together once you're better.

I couldn't bear to tell her the real reason why I wasn't attending my own graduation ceremony.

*

Baba didn't speak to me for several weeks. We'd pass each other in the hallway, or awkwardly bump into each other in the kitchen, but he wouldn't look at me.

Ahmed tiptoed around me. He didn't quite know what to say to me, so instead he tried to make me feel better through actions; buying me chocolates whenever he went out or getting me my favourite takeaway, a *shawarma* wrap and fries.

Knowing I'd been raped just deepened Saffa's anti-men sentiments and she'd walk about the house saying things within earshot of Baba like, "All men are perverts" and "I'm never getting married to an Arab."

One day Mum pulled her to the side. "Saffa, Baba's warned me to tell you that he's this close to sending you and Sara on a plane to live with your Aunt Mona in Egypt. And if it happens, you'll only have yourself to thank."

Saffa quickly stopped aggravating him.

Abdullah may have been almost ten years my junior, but he dealt with the situation by taunting me.

"You're a *sharmootah*." He smirked. "Going out with guys on your own? I can't believe my sister is a slut. I'm ashamed to call you my big sister"

"Shut your mouth," I yelled. "I'm your older sister. Have some respect."

"You've lost my respect." Abdullah laughed.

I walked past him, shoving him with my shoulder. I found Mum in the kitchen.

"Please do something about Abdullah," I said to her. "He keeps calling me a slut in Arabic. I'm gonna end up slapping him."

"I'll talk to him but I can't stop him. In Baba's eyes what Abdullah is saying is right," Mum said sadly.

"I don't care. I will knock him out if he talks to me like that again," I said before I went to my room, slamming the door shut behind me.

*

It was a quiet Friday afternoon and I was sat on my own watching TV when Mum and Baba entered the room. They were having another argument. Mum sat next to me, as Baba sat opposite us, and they continued to fight. I tried my best to block them out and continued watching a rerun of *The Simpsons*.

"How many bad things do you need to happen to our children before you give up your money and stupid position and take us back to England?" Mum shouted.

"We cannot go back to England. There's nothing left for us there. There's no house, no work," Baba argued.

"And whose fault is it that we don't have a house anymore? No one told you to sell it and then lose all your money in the stock market! And why? Because, as usual, you listened to one of your stupid Egyptian friends over your wife!"

Out of nowhere, my whole body started shaking violently. I tried to stop the shaking, but I had no control over it.

"What's wrong with you? Why are you shaking like this?" Baba asked, looking at me up and down.

"I can't control it!" I said, as tears raced down my face.

I felt like an invisible boa constrictor had wrapped itself around my torso, starving me of air. I hyperventilated, taking short and shallow breaths, and I felt like I was going to black out at any moment. Everything around me looked unreal.

"I think I'm going to faint," I said.

"Put your head between your legs and take slow deep breaths. In through your nose and out through your mouth," Mum said, putting her arm around my back.

It took a while for my breathing to return to normal and for the shaking to stop. All three of us were stunned. None of us had any idea what had just happened.

I started to find it hard to sleep at night. I'd get that same feeling of tightness in my chest the moment I laid down. I became hyper aware of my breathing, having to consciously breathe slowly in through my nose and out through my mouth to stop myself from hyperventilating.

A sense of terror would start from my belly and rise upwards, and I'd be convinced that I was about to die. The slow deep breathing sometimes worked and I'd eventually drop off to sleep, but in most cases I'd have to go downstairs to the living room and watch TV or read a book, until I'd fall asleep from exhaustion as the first of the day's sunshine became visible through our tinted windows.

I quickly learned that insomnia can make a person feel like they're going mad. For the first week or two, my body went into survival mode and somehow I managed to go about my normal day, surviving on an hour and a half of sleep. But I eventually reached breaking point. I'd give anything to be able to put my head down and get just three hours of sleep, but every time I tried to, my brain buzzed so loudly I could hear it in my ears. I felt so exhausted that I was physically sick. I wasn't suicidal, but death started to sound like a long, peaceful sleep.

One night, when my mind was again refusing to switch off and no amount of controlled breathing helped, I sat up and my mouth opened in a continuous wail, like the famous painting, *The Scream*.

I couldn't sleep. My mind kept bringing me back to that day in the desert, Nawaf pushing my neck down and refusing to stop.

My scream woke up both of my parents and they rushed into my bedroom.

"What's wrong, *ya Sara*?" Baba asked, for once looking genuinely worried. "Why are you crying so loudly?"

"I feel like I'm going mad!" I said between loud sobs, trying to control my breathing.

"You're going to wake the others up!" Mum whispered. "Come downstairs to the living room."

Baba went back to their bedroom and Mum led me by the hand downstairs where we sat beside each other on the sofa.

"I think you need to see a doctor," Mum said. "I'll tell Baba to find a psychiatrist in the morning."

"I'm not crazy!" I cried, and started to hyperventilate again.

"Sara, breathe," Mum said rubbing my back. "No one said you're crazy. You're not well. We need to get help for you."

Mum went back to their bedroom after sitting with me

for an hour. I stayed on the sofa with my head resting on the arm of the chair, and watched an early morning rerun of *Mad Men*. By 5am, I was growing sleepy and went back upstairs to my bedroom where I finally managed to go to sleep.

When I woke up three short hours later, Mum greeted me warmly as I walked into the living room.

"Baba's booking an appointment at the state psychiatry clinic for you," she said.

No way. I'd heard all sorts of horror stories about that place.

"I don't want to go!" I protested. "Can't I go to a private one? Baba gets medical insurance for us now!"

"One of the *amus* recommended a doctor there."

Typical. I was going to see someone just because they were a friend of a friend.

That evening when Baba came back from work, he handed me a white appointment card from the state hospital. I had an appointment with Dr El-Sayyid the next day in his evening clinic. Baba's friend had managed to tell Dr El-Sayyid that it was an emergency and we needed an urgent appointment. The doctor had overridden the usual system of going on a waiting list to get me the appointment. I guess being half Egyptian did have its perks.

Panic

On the way to my psychiatry appointment, Baba told me not to tell the psychiatrist about the rape. He was terrified that his friends in the local Egyptian community would find out and it would tarnish his reputation. I didn't reply and remained silent for the remainder of the journey.

The state hospital's psychiatry clinic was in a white, one-level building. The entrances and waiting rooms were segregated so Baba had to go through a separate entrance for men and we met back up in the lobby and checked in at the appointments desk. We separated again to go into the gender-segregated waiting rooms.

I much preferred the silent company of Baba to the women in the waiting room. Every single woman in that waiting room was dressed in a black *abaya* and *shayla*, some of them with their faces veiled. Even though some of the women's faces were veiled by their *niqabs*, you could see the sorrow in their eyes. One of them was rocking back and forth, muttering things to herself. Another one was sitting with her Indian house servant, staring blankly at the wall with her eyes open wide.

I longed for my name to be called out so I could get away from this waiting room that reeked of despair.

Finally, an Arab nurse dressed in a white skirt, with a matching nurse's jacket and white headscarf, called my name. Baba came out of the men's waiting room to join me. I would have preferred to have gone into the doctor's room on my own and have the freedom to express myself. I knew that with Baba sitting beside me, I'd have to talk in a mindful and controlled manner.

The nurse led us into Dr El-Sayyid's room. He sat behind a huge desk and had wispy grey hair that lined the sides of his balding head. He had a darkened mark in the middle of his forehead—a *sajdah* mark—*sajdah* being the Arabic word for 'prostration.' This mark was caused by years of prostrating during prayer on rough surfaces. Many Muslims considered a *sajdah* mark to be the ultimate sign of piety.

He motioned at the two chairs in front of his desk and Baba and I sat down. Baba and the psychiatrist started with pleasantries and then Dr El-Sayyid spoke to me in Arabic.

"Is it okay if I speak to you in English? My Arabic is still not 100 per cent," I asked.

"Speak in whatever language you like," he replied, smiling, and then he turned to Baba. "Do you mind, Dad, leaving me to talk to her alone, so that she may have some privacy?"

I turned to Baba whose eyes were wide but surprisingly he didn't protest. He quietly rose from his chair.

"I'll wait for you in the male waiting room."

I knew that even with Baba not there, I'd still need to mind what I told the psychiatrist. So I told him all about my insomnia and the physical symptoms I'd been experiencing, the feelings of panic, terror and doom, like I was about to die. I left out all the parts about Mum and Baba's fractured relationship and the rape.

"What it sounds like is a panic attack disorder," Dr El-Sayyid said after I'd finished talking. "Your body is reacting to anxiety by converting the emotions into physical symptoms."

He prescribed me an antidepressant called Seroxat which I was to take in the morning, and a tranquilliser before bedtime to help me sleep. He wanted to see me again in a week's time. I took the handwritten prescription, thanked him for his time and left his office, to find Baba waiting for me outside.

Seroxat was a small, oblong, white pill and the tranquilliser was a small, round, blue pill. I noticed when living in the Middle East that doctors wouldn't mention anything about side effects.

It was just as well that I'd finished university and it was now the summer holidays because the pills turned me into a zombie. I spent every day of that first week lying on my back on the floor in the living room with a cushion under my head. I couldn't stand up and walk without feeling like the whole room was spinning. My legs constantly buckled. I felt unable to focus on anything, and lost interest in everything from books to everyday conversations. I had no appetite. I only managed to eat one or two mouthfuls of dinner once a day.

Each hour felt like it crawled by, and when the night came and I took the tranquilliser, I slept for longer than I had for the past couple of months, but not without waking up feeling extremely nauseous.

On Friday evening, once the sun had fully set and the weather had become cooler, Mum and Baba decided to take me for a walk by the sea for a change of scenery. I had to walk with my arm linked in Mum's, and as we walked, with the sea on our right side and the busy highway and skyscrapers to our left, it felt like I was walking with virtual reality goggles on.

When I turned my head it felt like my sight wasn't properly connected to my brain, and it took a few seconds for my brain to catch up so objects would move in a jarred way across my field of vision.

On the car ride home, I was sitting in the passenger's seat next to Baba.

I should just throw myself out of the car.

The thought absolutely terrified me, yet at the same time I felt like I had to mentally restrain myself. I visualised myself pulling up the lock, opening the door, rolling out on to the dark grey tarmac and being run over by a car.

When I got home, I changed into my pyjamas and went to the toilet. As I stood over the sink and washed my hands, I looked at my reflection in the mirror, unable to recognise myself. It felt like the person staring back at me was a stranger. Was I going mad? I felt worse than I had before taking the medication.

I'd really hoped that the horrible urge to throw myself out of Baba's moving car had been a one-off but the thoughts continued. I became terrified of using knives, afraid that I'd lose control and stab myself in the thigh, cut a slit across my belly, or worse, hurt one of my siblings.

I couldn't deal with it any longer, and I told Mum about these terrible thoughts. Panicked, she called Gran in England, who was a retired medical secretary. When Mum came off the phone, she went to the kitchen cupboard where she kept all the medicines, took the box of Seroxat and tranquilliser pills, and threw them in the bin.

"You're not taking this rubbish anymore," she yelled. "Stupid Baba taking you to another useless Egyptian doctor. Do you know what Gran just told me? She told me to throw away those pills right now because in America they've been taken off the shelves after causing loads of teenagers to commit suicide!"

I never went back to see Dr El-Sayyid. And since I'd been taking the pills for only a week, I was fortunate enough not to suffer from any withdrawal effects. But my anxiety was still there, and I needed to do something about it.

Repercussions

Baba spoke to his line manager at work about the rape. He and his line manager had been friends since we were in England, and they were close. He was one of the few people Baba trusted. He'd called Baba in for a one-to-one meeting because he was concerned about him. He'd noticed that Baba hadn't been his cheery self at work, and was quiet and depressed. Baba broke down and told him what had happened to me.

His line manager turned out to be friends with the chief prosecutor in the country. Baba hadn't bothered to ask me if I wanted to report what happened with Nawaf to the police. He went ahead and agreed with his line manager to speak about what had happened to me with the chief prosecutor; the most important man in the country's judicial system. However, the chief prosecutor came back and said he couldn't open a case.

"Baba tried for you Sara," Mum said, relaying what had happened with the chief prosecutor to me while sat on my bed. "Despite everything Baba might have said in anger, he tried to get justice for you. But the chief prosecutor told

Baba's manager that because you willingly went out with this man—"

"For a date!"

"I know but in the eyes of a jury by consenting to go out with a man who is not your husband anything that happens afterwards is your fault. He said you could even end up being punished under the laws of *zina*, illicit pre-marital relationships, and be sent to prison. The chief prosecutor said if this man is from the royal family then he'll get away with it. He told Baba's manager to tell Baba that he will keep this scandal a secret and that Baba should thank God that you're still alive."

I began to hyperventilate. Nawaf was going to get away with raping me.

"Breathe Sara, in through your nose out and through your mouth," Mum said, holding my hand.

"I need to go to the toilet," I said quickly and leapt off my bed.

I rushed to the bathroom and splashed my face with cold water. I decided there and then that I wouldn't let Nawaf ruin my life, nor would I let this panic disorder beat me.

I started using a mantra which I would repeat to myself, both aloud and in my head. "You're going to be okay. You're strong," and it really did help.

I sat at the family computer and searched for a list of all the psychiatrists, psychologists and counsellors in the country. I found a Lebanese lady who was a psychiatrist at a private hospital not far from where I lived who had lots of positive reviews. It would cost 250 riyals which was equivalent to £50 a session, but Baba would get that money reimbursed by the medical insurance company. I told Mum and Baba about her at dinnertime that evening, and Baba agreed to give me the money I needed to see her.

Dr Hala had a kind, round face, framed by a light-blue hijab which complemented her baby-blue blouse.

"How can I help you?" she asked, once I'd finished. filling out my medical history. "Please know that everything you tell me is in complete confidence. It's my job as a doctor to listen to you with no judgement."

So I told her everything. The family move from London to the Gulf, the tumultuous relationship between Mum, Baba and my siblings, my naïve plan to fall in love and get married to a Gulf man, and how it had culminated in rape and a panic attack disorder. When I got to the part about the rape and how Nawaf was from the royal family, she raised her hand and I stopped talking.

"Can I ask you if you have a mobile phone?"

"Yes."

"We need to take out both the SIM card and the battery from both of our phones."

I didn't question her and did as she said.

"This is because the police tap into phones," she explained to me. She then let me continue talking.

"I'm not a virgin anymore, no one will ever marry me," I said, as I finished telling her what had happened that day in the desert. I burst into tears and she handed me her box of tissues, her face full of genuine concern.

"I'm not a psychologist, but many young Arab women come to me just to talk. And many of them have been through similar experiences to yours. Some of them even lost their virginity by choice. But they've all got married. My advice?

Just don't tell any man you get to know from now on about the rape. There's no way he'll know whether or not you're a virgin. Keep it a secret."

I wiped my eyes with a tissue and nodded.

"At the stage you're at with your panic attacks, I do think medication will help for the short-term. I'm going to prescribe you an antidepressant called Faverin. You had side effects from the Seroxat?" Dr Hala pulled her prescription pad across her desk. I nodded my head. "Okay, well let me know if this causes you any problems."

When Dr Hala handed over my prescription, I thanked her and stood up to leave.

"Sara, have you been tested for sexually transmitted diseases?" she asked.

It hadn't even crossed my mind. I thought STDs were a thing that only people in the West got from having multiple sexual partners before marriage.

"No," I said. "Do I need to?"

"Yes, it's better you do it sooner rather than later. In order for it to be covered by the medical insurance you'll need to see a doctor in a gynaecology department. If I request the tests you might have to pay for them."

"Okay, I'll get booked in."

Since I was already in the hospital, and the gynaecology department was on the same floor, I decided to go and see a gynaecologist as a walk-in patient.

I walked up to the reception desk and registered myself.

"Are there any gynaecologists available?"

The receptionist looked at her computer. "There's Dr Amani and Dr Mohammed."

"Oh, can I see the female doctor please?"

"Of course. Dr Amani has one patient in front of you, so take a seat and wait."

I sat down and noticed seven other women waiting. That was strange. Why would they all want to see a male gynaecologist if there was a female one available?

I didn't have to wait long before an Arab nurse came to the waiting room and called out my name. I followed her through a dark and narrow white corridor to Dr Amani's office. I guessed from the doctor's name that she was Egyptian, and my guess was spot-on.

"How can I help you, dear?" Dr Amani asked me in Arabic.

"Six months ago I was raped and I would like to have a check-up and get tested for STDs."

"Was it someone you know?" she asked.

"It was someone I was getting to know for the purpose of marriage," I replied, not using the word "dated" because I knew it might come with disapproval.

"Did he not do it lovingly or was it violent?" she asked. "Why didn't you marry him?"

My mouth dropped open.

Did I not just tell her that I'd been raped? What part of being raped could be loving and gentle? And why would I want to marry my rapist?

"Do you mind if I take a look at you?" she asked, when I didn't respond.

She called in a nurse who showed me to the elevated examination bed on the side, and drew the curtain around me as I took off my *abaya*, my trousers and my knickers, and draped them over a chair.

"Lie on your back, and bend your knees," the nurse instructed, taking out a white blanket from beneath the bed. "Scoot yourself all the way down to the end so the doctor can examine you."

The room was cold and my naked thighs shivered under the blanket. I heard the sound of rubber gloves snapping as Dr Amani put them on and came over to examine me.

She turned on the light overhead and prodded me down below.

"Yes unfortunately, your hymen is fully broken. I advise that you have a smear test, but we can do that on another day. You can get dressed now."

She left me to put my clothes back on. Once I had gotten dressed, I walked back over and sat on the chair across the desk from her.

"Here are the medical test request forms." She handed them to me as I stood.

"Thanks," I said, but I had no intention of coming back to see this backward doctor again after the rubbish she had come out with about marrying my rapist. I would have to see another gynaecologist and get my smear test done with them.

Over the next couple of days I was back at the hospital to do the various blood tests and submit my urine sample. Some of the results would be ready in a few days; some would take two to three weeks as they didn't have the facilities to test for things like herpes at that time so the samples got sent to Germany.

I decided I'd just wait until all the results were back before going back to the hospital. Unfortunately, the test for herpes wasn't covered by insurance and it would cost 1000 riyals (£200). I had to ask Mum to ask Baba for the money.

"Can you lie and tell him it's for something else?" I begged Mum.

"I can but he's going to find out because the insurance company will email him the invoice," Mum replied sadly. "I'm sorry Sara. I promise you I won't let him do or say anything to you."

When I asked Mum the following day how he'd reacted when he handed her the money she said, "He says you're a ruined woman, and that no one will ever marry you. Don't believe him. One day we'll go back to England and you'll find yourself a lovely man."

I had an excruciating three-week wait for the results. The Faverin hadn't kicked in yet, so my anxiety levels were through the roof. Every day during those three weeks I imagined that I'd go back to the hospital and receive the bad news that I had an STD. I feared herpes the most, as I knew that was the one that stuck around forever. I made sure to pray every one of my five prayers on time and made *du'aa* after *du'aa* that Allah would forgive me and let my test results come back negative.

When I called the hospital, they confirmed that my results were ready. I went back and asked again at the reception for the names of the gynaecologists that were available. There was a different female doctor on shift that morning. Her name was Dr Salma. I sighed with relief that it wasn't Dr Amani and asked to see her.

As I waited for my turn, I quietly asked Allah for forgiveness, over and over again. I had once watched an Islamic lecture on YouTube and in it the sheikh had said that if a calamity had befallen you that the best thing was to repent to Allah as often as possible, and then Allah would remove it.

Dr Salma was a middle-aged woman from Iraq, who ended every sentence with *eyni*, an Iraqi word which was a shortened way of saying 'the apple of my eye' in Arabic. When she asked if I was married and I told her very briefly that I'd been raped, her face broke into an expression of heartache.

"I'm so sorry this happened to you. This man took advantage of you and your trust. I believe God will grant you someone one day who will make up for all that you've suffered. This was not your fault."

I decided right then that if I needed a smear test, I would ask her to do it. I told her about the intrusive and personal questions Dr Amani had asked and how she had asked me why I hadn't married my rapist. She frowned but didn't say anything against her colleague. I could tell from the look on her face though that she was not impressed with Dr Amani.

Dr Salma opened the dark pink cardboard file that was lying on her desk and pulled out three pieces of paper that were at the very front, her forehead furrowed as she read my test results.

I prayed under my breath. *Allah the Greatest please forgive me. I repent to you.*

She finally looked up, put the papers down, smiled and said, "Don't worry. Everything came back normal. You don't have any STDs."

"*Alhamdulillah*, all praise and thanks belong to God," I replied. "*Alhamdulillah* a thousand times."

Grown Woman

I continued to see Dr Hala for almost a year to help with my panic attacks. They lessened in frequency until they almost became a distant memory and I eventually got my sleep back.

Dr Hala encouraged me to start applying for jobs so I spent five hours a day searching online for vacancies and filling out applications. I swear applying for a job became a job itself. I signed up to dozens of free job-hunting websites and contacted local recruitment agencies, but months passed and I didn't get a single interview.

I then took a more aggressive approach and called companies directly, even printing copies of my CV and going around the city in a taxi, handing in my CV to companies in person. This more direct approach was a complete waste of time because I'd just get told to go back to the company's website and apply online.

Once I came close to getting a job as a research assistant at a Think Tank that had recently opened. It was just the kind of job I'd been hoping for with my Political Science degree, and after weeks of being on tenterhooks I'd found out that

I needed final approval from their HR manager. In the end I didn't get it. They decided it should go to a Gulf applicant on the basis of prioritising Gulf applicants first. The country had started implementing a policy of nationalisation of jobs and employers were encouraged to give the locals priority over other nationalities.

I had no desire to date guys anymore. It had been a year since I'd last been at one of Heba's parties. My secret life of dating and partying was over.

Heba and I still spoke every day on the phone, and occasionally Baba would let me go out with her to see a movie or eat out, on the condition that he or Mum watched her pick me up and drop me off at our front door.

"It's been a while since you've come to a party or been on a date, Sara," Heba mentioned as we sat in a Starbucks one afternoon drinking frappes. "What's the deal? Are you like proper religious now?"

"It's not that," I replied, taking another sip of my drink. "I'm not any more religious than I was before. I'm just tired of guys and their bullshit. And my dad's become really strict now about me being out late and sleeping over, even if it's on the premise of me going to a wedding."

Heba raised an eyebrow. "Ever since our last semester at uni you've not been the same. I know something's happened. It's hurting me that you don't trust me enough to tell me."

I swallowed my frappe guiltily and looked down.

"I do trust you. I've got nothing to tell. My life's the same as it's always been. Controlled, restricted, no way out. Can't find a job. Can't get married. I'll be stuck living with my dad the dictator till they day he dies."

"You're young! Don't be so defeated! You can't give up on your life. You're gonna start coming out and having fun with me and my friends, even if I have to get the whole country to lie to your dad for you."

Heba prodded me in the shoulder and I started to laugh.

In 2012, at the age of twenty-three, I finally got a job as a secretary for a director at a big real estate company. But before Heba and I could celebrate, I had to get my work permit.

In the Gulf, if you're a woman you need both the permission of the government and either your father or your husband—if you're married—in order to be able to work.

When I received my job offer, I needed a letter of no objection from Baba before I could start the process of applying for a work permit from the government. If he objected to me working, I wouldn't be allowed by the government to work in the country. So, I was stuck under Baba's thumb unless I got married, something that had become very unlikely now that I no longer owned a hymen.

"My daughter, a secretary?" Baba said, turning up his nose. "Is that the best job you could find?"

"It's the *only* job I could find," I replied. "Baba, it's been years since I graduated. Please let me accept the offer."

Baba sighed. "Very well. But let me remind you about the rules. If I allow you to work in a mixed environment and I discover you're messing around with men, I'll keep you at home."

I rolled my eyes and he caught me.

"Go get me pen and paper *yalla* before I change my mind."

I may have been spending my days filling out my Gulf

boss's visa applications, fetching his lunch and helping him pick out ceramic tiling for his new bathroom, but it just felt so good to be going out every day, interacting with people, and getting a nice sum of money in my very own bank account at the end of each month for it.

I bought myself a smartphone with my first pay check.

Working up all the courage I had, I told Baba, "I've bought a mobile phone. I need it. I'm a working woman and my boss needs to be able to get in touch with me."

"Yes, very well then, you can have a phone for work," he said.

I could finally give Heba her phone back.

"*Mabrook*, congratulations, I guess!" Heba laughed when I handed back her phone.

Now that I had a proper job, I could finally afford to buy myself some decent clothes, instead of the baggy trousers, long tunics and maxi skirts that had to be approved by Baba since I was buying clothes with his money.

I thought back to why I'd decided to wear a black *abaya* and *shayla* like the Gulf women. I'd wanted to assimilate into their society so badly so that I could marry a Gulf man. Now that dream was over, there was no reason why I couldn't take off my *abaya* and wear nice clothes.

I sat trawling through Pinterest with Saffa.

"What do you think? Shall I stop wearing my *abaya* and start wearing coloured *shaylas* instead of black ones?"

"Oh my God, yes!" she exclaimed. "Shopping trip!"

Several new shopping malls complete with IMAX cinemas had popped up across the country and Saffa and I spent one Saturday afternoon trawling though shop after shop until I'd bought myself an entire new wardrobe.

When I got home, we put all my black *abayas* and *shaylas* into black bin bags.

"What are you doing?" Mum asked when she saw the black bin bags.

"I've got some old clothes I want to give to charity," I replied, tying the bags up.

"Let me have a look," she said, and opened up one of the bags. "Sara! Your *abayas*! Why are you throwing them away?"

"I don't need them, Mum. I'm not trying to be someone I'm not anymore."

The next time I went out with Heba, she squealed when she saw me without an *abaya*.

"Finally!" she exclaimed. "I'm so proud. What did your dad say though?"

"Nothing. He took one look at me going out to work without one and all he said was to put a long cardigan over my blouse and cover my bum."

"Oh God, he's not going to start with that again is he? The way he did before you wore *abayas*?"

"I don't know. But maybe I'll start answering him back. I'm buying clothes with my money now, not his."

"What about your *hijab*? You might as well take it off. I mean, you take it off when you go to parties with me."

I knew that removing my *hijab* would be a step too far for me but she was right. I was still living a double life. Why did I wear the *hijab*? Did I actually believe in it? Deep down, I knew I was only wearing it to keep Baba happy, not because I actually understood it, or was convinced of its necessity.

Once, when Saffa questioned the *hijab*, Baba said, "When a woman takes off her *hijab* she tears down the relationship between herself and Allah. Allah will be angry with her and she'll be sent to Hell. Muslim women are precious diamonds, and what do you do when you have something precious? You cover it to protect it."

Who was he to judge who went to Heaven and Hell? I was no longer convinced of his reasoning, but I didn't have the balls just yet to tell him, or to take my *shayla* off. I needed more time to work up the courage.

Adulthood

It was the midst of the Arab Spring and countries across North Africa and the Middle East were in full revolution. Civil war had broken out in Libya and Syria, and Baba had become increasingly busy at work organising news coverage. We rarely saw him. We didn't mind since it meant we could be more relaxed at home.

Mum didn't feel under pressure to cook him his traditional Egyptian dinners. With him out, Mum, Saffa, Ahmed, Abdullah and I would spend our evenings sat together around the TV screen, watching American movies on Showtime, not having to change the channel when a kissing scene came on, or being told that we couldn't watch the movie at all because of the swear words.

We took full advantage of the fact that Baba was having to work late most nights. Ahmed would stay out with his friends all night and come back in the early hours of the morning, and I would go out to parties with Heba on an almost weekly basis. I pushed my curfew from 10pm to midnight and Baba wasn't around to find out and object. Either he'd given up on us, or he'd decided that the Arab Spring was more important.

Abdullah, however, was becoming a problem, and not in the way Ahmed and I had imagined. Saffa, Ahmed and I had waited to see how Abdullah would change when he became a teenager. Was he going to start going out with other boys his age and misbehaving the way Ahmed had at the age of fourteen? Was Abdullah going to start disobeying Baba and answering him back?

He did the exact opposite. Abdullah made friends with a group of Palestinian boys whose grandparents fled the Israeli Occupation in 1948 and settled all over the Gulf. Some of the Palestinian men were extremely misogynistic, and honour killings and domestic abuse were not uncommon in the Palestinian villages they'd left.

The abusive ways of their fathers trickled down to the boys and they were clapped on the back by their elders for taking a firm stance against their sisters. The boys even had the cheek to dictate to their mothers and older sisters where they could or couldn't go, and how they could or couldn't dress. Abdullah was being massively influenced.

"Why is there never a cooked lunch ready for me when I come home from school like the Palestinian boys?" Abdullah asked Mum when he got back from school one day.

Mum laughed at him.

"I'm being serious!" Abdullah snapped. "My friends shout at their mothers if they don't make them a decent cooked meal."

"Well I'm not their mum and I won't have my son telling me what to do," Mum said with her hands on her hips. "I've had enough of taking orders from Baba, so you must be out of your mind if you think I'm going to take orders from you!"

"I hate having a white mum!" Abdullah mumbled, but Mum heard him.

"Go to your room! I don't want to see your face for the rest of the evening!" Mum shouted, and Abdullah stormed upstairs scowling and muttering things under his breath.

"The bloody cheek," Mum said, turning to me.

Saffa, who was lying on the sofa with her feet propped up on the armrest, raised her head. "You should complain to Baba. It's not fair. Me, Ahmed and Sara would get hit with the wooden spoon for being rude to you and Abdullah gets away with it."

But later at the dining table when Mum complained to Baba while Abdullah was still sulking in his bedroom, Baba shrugged.

"I'd rather Abdullah be influenced by the Palestinian boys than be like Ahmed, influenced by the West."

"Baba, that's not fair!" I said. "You didn't let us get away with this behaviour. I'm not telling you to beat him, just tell him off for being rude to his mother and his older sisters!"

"I'm old and I'm tired of problems. Give me a break please," Baba said sternly, and he resumed eating his dinner.

*

"What do you think Baba would do if I took off my *hijab*?" I asked Mum casually as I laid out vine leaves on the kitchen worktable for her to stuff with rice and roll into little parcels called *wara' enab*.

Mum stopped stuffing the vine leaves and looked at me. "You've lost the plot. Are you trying to kill your father?"

"It's just a question, Mum."

"No it isn't. I know you. You're thinking about taking it off, aren't you?"

"I'm tired of living a lie. I don't believe it's compulsory or necessary. I'm an adult. I should be able to make my own life decisions."

"That's if we were living in England, my love. In the Gulf you're a child in the eyes of the law until you get married."

"What if I don't get married Mum? I'm tired of Baba ruling us as if we're a Gulf family. We're not. We're British. Just because we have to live here doesn't mean we need to copy their rules."

"As long as you live in his house, you have to follow Baba's rules."

"Okay, I'll move out then."

"You're really talking crazy now! He'll never allow it."

"Mum, I'm not a virgin. As long as we live in the Arab world no one is going to ever marry me. I might as well live free and independent. I'm not going to allow myself to wind up like one of these Arab women who are in their forties, unmarried and still living in their dad's house, following their dad's rules."

Taking off my *hijab* was one of the most dangerous decisions I could make, but I decided to go ahead and do it. Would Baba disown me? If he did, at least I earned enough money now to support myself. Would he cancel my visa and send me to Egypt or the UK? I was a grown woman, surely now I could run away and start my own life again from scratch?

This was it. I was going to do it.

I tiptoed down the stairs dressed in tapered beige trousers and a black and white, long-sleeved, polka-dot blouse, minus my *hijab*. Heba was picking me up for dinner. I was ready to face Baba, ready for a fight. My core muscles were braced and my body was hardened just in case I was to receive a blow from him.

"I give up," he said when he saw me, waving a hand in the air dramatically. "I've spent all your lives trying to raise you as good Muslim children. I brought you to this country to save you from the problems in London—the bullying in schools, the drugs, the alcohol, the violence. And this is how you repay me? You're an adult. I've done my job. Just make sure you're ready to be questioned by Allah."

Saffa and Mum looked at each other, mouths open in shock.

I couldn't believe it had been that easy! My heart still pounded violently inside my ribcage, and I felt my brow sweat with nerves. For a moment, I doubted myself and thought about rushing upstairs to put a long cardigan over the top of my clothes and grab a *shayla*. But I picked up my handbag, put on my ballet flats by the front door, and walked out without my *hijab*.

"You're really a *sharmootah* now," Abdullah said as I walked past him. "If Baba won't say it, I will. I'm ashamed to have you as my sister." He gave me a look of disgust. He looked like a mini version of Baba.

"What did you say?" I hissed. I jabbed Abdullah in the chest. "Say that again."

Abdullah's mouth was tense but he didn't say a word.

When I realised how easy that had been with Baba, I started to become even more daring. Blouses and tops started to get tucked into the trousers instead of being left untucked, so they no longer covered my bum. Long sleeves were then replaced by T-shirts.

Even though Baba claimed to have given up on me, my teenage brother Abdullah took his place. Every time I made my way to the front door to go out, Abdullah would stop me.

"Where do you think you're going?" he would ask accusingly.

"I'm going out with Heba. Why are you asking?"

"I know you're lying. I bet you're going out with guys and that's why you're dressed like that. If I could beat you like my Palestinian friends beat their sisters I would."

I grabbed him by the arm and he winced. "Don't you dare talk to me like that! How many times do I have to tell you? You have no right to ask me where I'm going or tell me how I should be dressing. Do you understand me?"

When he didn't respond I gripped his arm tighter and Abdullah eventually nodded.

"Keep your mouth shut from now on," I said and with that I stormed out of the house.

Bat-Shit Crazy

It felt good not having to live a double life anymore. I put on a white dress that had very short sleeves and the hem only just skimmed my knees. I took out a brand new red lipstick. It had been years since I'd worn red lipstick in public. Was I brave enough to go out dressed like this? Should I wear red lipstick? It would look perfect with this dress.

There was a cocktail party that evening that I'd been invited to by Heba's circle of friends. One of them was DJing at the event and we were going along to show him some support. I thought Baba had gone out before I made my exit, but I'd timed it wrong. It was Ahmed who had slammed the front door shut on his way out, not Baba, who was very much still at home, sat on the living room sofa in his pyjamas.

When he saw me stood in the corridor, my hair, which had been recently dyed golden brown cascading down my shoulders, the frills of my Marilyn Monroe-esque dress swishing above my knees under the cool air of the AC unit, and worst of all, the Hollywood Red Maybelline lipstick coating my lips, he went bat-shit crazy.

"You've gone too far this time!" he shouted, and stood up. "You took off your *hijab* and I said nothing, even though it was my right to make you wear it or force you to stay at home. But where do you think you're going dressed like a *sharmootah*? Do you think I'm stupid? That I believe that you have an engagement party or a wedding every weekend?"

I knew he was waiting for me to answer him back or cry, but I didn't say a word. This made him even angrier.

"I hate you!" he shouted, making me jump. "You've made me hate you!"

And I think he meant it. I could see it in his face. His upper lip quivered in disgust; his eyebrows furrowed in anger. His eyes pierced mine, full of hatred. I didn't know what to do next because Heba was already outside waiting for me in her car.

"*Khalas*, that's it, you're not going out," Baba said, waving his hand dramatically to signify that he'd had enough of me.

"But Baba, Heba's already waiting for me outside."

"To hell with Heba! Tell her what you want! You're not leaving this house, and if you do, don't return here!" he yelled.

In that split second, I knew I had a momentous decision to make. If I defied him further I risked the possibility of being kicked out, which to be honest, I wasn't afraid of anymore, as I had enough money to financially support myself. It would only become an issue if he followed through with his threat of cancelling my visa. Or I could submit, call Heba to apologise for dragging her all the way out here and go upstairs to my bedroom and sulk all evening like a teenager.

Wobbling over to the door of Heba's car, I could barely hold myself together before I sat in the front passenger seat, closed the car door and started to cry, ruining my eye make-up.

"What's wrong?" Heba asked, holding onto my hand.

"Let's get away from here first and then I'll tell you. I don't want my dad to look out of the window and see us sitting here," I told her, and she drove off.

As Heba drove aimlessly, allowing me time to talk, I told her how Baba had told me face-to-face that he hated me because of what I was wearing, and he told me not to come back home if I defied him and went out in my white dress and red lipstick.

"I'm really sorry to say this babe but your dad is crazy!" Heba exclaimed. "You don't need to worry. You know my parents will have you at ours in an instant. Stay with us for as long as you want."

"Oh, I couldn't impose—"

"Don't be ridiculous! Where else are you going to go? This isn't a country where you can sleep on the streets and you can't afford to sleep at a hotel every night."

"Okay then. Thank you so much. I'm going to have to go home at some point to collect my things. I don't want to face him," I groaned.

"Let's figure that out later. Do you still want to go to the party? We don't have to go if you don't feel like it. We can just chill at my place."

I was really glad she said that, because it was now the last thing I wanted to do. We went back to hers and watched episodes of *RuPaul's Drag Race*. As much as I tried to relax, focus on the show and not think about what was going to happen next, I couldn't. I just kept visualising going back home to pack my things and getting into a massive fight with Baba.

At around 11pm I saw Baba's name flashing across the screen of my phone.

"Shit, it's my dad. I don't want to pick up."

"Give it to me," Heba said, holding out her hand.

"I'm scared he'll shout at you instead of me."

"I've got this," Heba said, and she snatched my phone out of my hands.

Heba was silent as she let Baba do the talking and I could hear his deep voice booming out of the speaker, but was unable to make out what he was saying. After letting him speak for what felt like forever, my heart beating so hard and fast I could have sworn you could have seen it pumping through my skin, she managed to get a word in.

"If you want her to come home you have to swear by Allah that you won't shout at her or lay a finger on her," she said.

I heard more deep noises from my phone and watched Heba nod.

"Thank you so much *amu*, we're just going to eat dinner and I'll drop her home." And she hung up.

We listened to the outdated tracks being played on the country's only English radio station in silence on the drive back to my place. As Heba pulled up in front of my house I felt like I was going to be sick.

"I'm sure it'll be okay, your dad swore by Allah, and he's religious so he won't break his oath. Text me to let me know everything's okay."

I hugged her tight. I didn't want to let go and leave her car. Eventually I allowed myself to leave her embrace.

"Thank you for always being there," I said.

"Don't be silly, that's what friends are for," Heba replied, and waved me off.

I wished deep down that she would come inside with me,

but felt too silly to ask her. As she drove away, I stood watching, wishing I was still next to her in her flashy BMW.

I turned around and faced the pathway that led to my front door. I stood there for about five minutes, trying to delay going in as long as I could. It had just gone past midnight and I prayed to Allah that he'd gone to bed already, but it was the weekend and I knew the chances of that were slim, as he usually stayed up on the weekend to watch football.

I slipped my house key into the lock of the front door, opening it ever so slowly, and gently pushed the door open. I locked it quietly behind me. I crept along the hallway, and sure enough, Baba was still awake sitting in the living room, watching football just as I'd expected, cursing in Arabic every time his team missed a goal. Totally un-Islamic.

I expected him to stop when he saw me and call me in to restart the fight he tried to instigate earlier, but he ignored me as I crept upstairs to my bedroom. He kept his promise to Heba. But I knew that even if I wasn't going to be screamed at or hit, at the very least I would get a lecture in the next day or two.

Perfect Arab Daughter

"Sara, do you know anyone who's looking for a flat? My flatmate's moving out and I need a new one," asked a girl at work who worked in our marketing team. We were stood in the staff kitchen making coffee.

"I'll ask around," I promised.

"That would be great, thank you."

How about I take that second bedroom for myself? Don't be crazy! Baba would never say yes.

I couldn't stop thinking about moving out and finally being independent. I was getting anxious that if I didn't act quickly my colleague would find someone else.

I tried my best to avoid Baba. I told Mum that I wasn't feeling hungry at dinner time so I wouldn't have to sit at the dining table with him and stare at my food for an entire half an hour in order to avoid eye contact. But after they were done eating dinner, Mum called me down to wash the dishes.

As I stood trying to scrub burned rice off the bottom of a pan, I felt Baba's giant shadow looming behind me.

"When you've finished the washing up, come to the living room. We need to talk," he said.

"Okay," I said quietly.

I felt dizzy as I tried to finish washing up, knowing that it was pointless trying to delay things as I would have to face him eventually.

I dried my hands on a tea towel and walked into the living room, seating myself as far away from him as possible. He was reading one of his books on Islamic law over a cup of red tea. The giant hardcover book made a big thud as he shut it and put it down on the coffee table in front of him. Whatever he said, I wasn't going to let it get to me.

In one ear, out the other, Sara.

"Do you really have no shame telling Heba I'd beat you?"

I tried to look anywhere except his eyes, which were full of resentment. Instead, I kept looking at the giant black mole that was hanging off his leg. It reminded me of the famous *Austin Powers* mole scene where Austin couldn't take his eyes off a secret agent's giant black mole instead of focusing on their conversation. Remembering that made me want to laugh, so I bit the insides of my cheeks.

"Do you think this is funny?" Baba asked, raising his voice.

I shook my head.

"I've sacrificed everything for you and your siblings. I brought you here to an Islamic country to give you the best life. I paid for you to go to good schools and universities. And everything you're doing is the cause of my illness. My high blood pressure and diabetes are through the roof because of you. If I die, it'll be your fault," he said, clutching at his white vest with both of his hands.

I stood up. "No, you didn't come to this country because it was Islamic, you came because you got a good job offer and you thought you were going to be the big boss. You paid for me to go to a private high school here but I hated it. You didn't pay for me to go to university, I got a scholarship! And I didn't cause your diabetes and high blood pressure, you've got those because of your crappy eating habits and lack of physical activity."

Baba was speechless. I readied myself to get slapped. If he touched me, I was going to make a run for it.

But instead of hitting me, Baba sighed. "It's a shame, Sara, a real shame. I used to be so proud of you. When you used to win Qur'an competitions and the teachers at Arabic School used to praise you and tell me how they wished they had a daughter as good as you." Baba shook his head. "I don't even want to look at you now. Another father would have killed you after everything you've done. If we lived in Saudi Arabia, you would have been called an adulterer and got stoned to death."

I felt my eyes well up with tears. I couldn't cry or he'd win.

"That day with that man in the tent, why didn't you fight back?" Baba continued. "It would have been better for you to fight him, even if it meant he killed you. You would have died a martyr."

And that's when it hit me. He just didn't care. He'd rather I was killed than raped. I wasn't the perfect Arab daughter, but why couldn't I have a father who hugged me and held my hand, who accepted me for who I was and who loved me unconditionally?

I wiped the tears away angrily. "I've had enough too. I want to leave. I have a female colleague at work who has a spare bedroom and I want to take it."

"Go on *yalla*, leave. *Ma'a salama*, goodbye," Baba said, waving his hand dismissively.

So the next day, I left.

"So, five years have passed since that day when I packed my belongings and left home. And here I am, a couple of heartbreaks, a marriage and a divorce later. "

"What made you finally come back to London after you left your father's home?" Sophie asked.

It was the last day of our interview and we were seated in my gorgeous flat. I looked out of my window, sipping from my cup of tea as I looked out at the busy main road in Oval, watching the red double-decker buses and black cabs roll by.

"The day I left Baba's house I thought I was free, but I wasn't, not until the day I boarded a plane with my one-way ticket and left the shackles of the guardianship system behind me. Not long after I left, Saffa moved back to London and she's studying art, just like she's always wanted to. Ahmed came a few months later and he is doing well as a personal trainer. Mum continues to live with Baba. She plans to move home as soon as Abdullah has graduated from university."

"And your father?"

I smiled. "Baba is quiet nowadays. The day I left he changed. He loosened the reigns on my siblings. Maybe he was afraid to lose them the way he'd lost me. Maybe it took me leaving to make him realise that you'll lose your children by behaving like a dictator. We didn't talk for years. Mum would let me know how Baba was doing and vice versa. Then finally one Sunday, as I sat eating my breakfast, a number flashed on my phone. . ."

It was Baba.

"Sara?" His voice was so quiet. I felt my eyes well up.

"*Salam alaikum*, peace be upon you, Baba."

"*Wa alaikum asalam* and may peace be upon you. Mum told me you put your *hijab* back on. Is this true?"

"Yes, it's true."

"Every single night I prayed Allah would guide you back to the right path and He has answered my prayers! You don't know how happy I am. You're now my daughter again. I love you."

It was the first time Baba had ever told me he loved me. And it was all because I had put my *hijab* back on. I could break his heart and tell him I'd put my *hijab* back on because I wanted to, not because of him. But I decided not to. By forgiving him, I had finally set myself free.

"I love you too, Baba. You take care of yourself now," I said, and then I hung up.

*

My BBC documentary airs next week. I've asked Sophie to send me the video file so I can send it to Mum. Saffa and Ahmed are coming over to watch it with me. Even Abdullah said he'll tune in.

"Will Baba watch it?" I asked Mum over FaceTime.

"I'm sorry Sara, he said he can't," Mum said softly.

I spend my days writing. I write about the Middle East, female genital mutilation, domestic abuse and honour killings. My articles get published in some of the most well-known newspapers. I sit on panels at conferences and speak about gender justice and I get invited on to radio shows to talk about feminism. I had to wait a long time for it, but I'm finally doing the job I always wanted to do.

I'm using the opportunities tell my story, and to tell other women's stories, and make sure they get out there. They get read, listened to and known.

When I moved home I finally got the spiritual freedom I needed to soul search. I had access to uncensored articles and books, and my love of Islam was reignited.

For the first time in my life I could read English translations of the Qur'an and *hadith* for myself, instead of having it trickled down to me through Baba, never knowing whether what he was telling me was correct, or his own version of things.

A wealth of Islamic resources were available to me, instead of the Wahabbi books that were printed by the government that encouraged women to cover their faces and to stay with their husbands even if their husbands beat them.

I was enlightened and reawakened, reading books by T J Winters, Muhammed Abdul Haleem and Adil Salahi. I devoured books by Leila Ahmed, Asma Barlas and Fatima Mernissi that explored women's rights in Islam. I found out why my dad thought the way he did and the way the male Arab population in the Middle East at large think. There was nothing wrong with Islam. Islam gave women all their rights, even more so in some cases than other religions I had studied.

Divine Islamic law made both married and unmarried women owners of properties and wealth over 1400 years ago, whereas married women only became proprietors by law in England in 1882. The problem lay with the way Arab men mixed their culture with religion and wrongfully claimed certain rules were part of Islam when they weren't.

I separated my religion, which was not to blame for the way Baba had treated me, from the Arab culture, which was obsessed with a woman's reputation and honour, placing a woman's worth on the presence of her hymen.

I learned how the Prophet Muhammed, peace be upon him, was pro women's rights. He never made a decision without consulting the women in his life first, and his wives were active participants in society. It was other men in his society who had an issue with the way Prophet Muhammed treated women like equals.

I found out that the Prophet Muhammed fought for women to be treated justly and to have the right to divorce their husbands if they wanted to. He would tell men over and over again to treat their wives and daughters well. The Prophet Muhammed envisioned a society where men and women would be equals and treat each other with respect. He was way ahead of his time.

The women of the first Muslim community were bold, knowledgeable and fierce, who spoke up if the face of injustice and were respected by their male peers. They were the community's first teachers and men went to them to gain Islamic knowledge.

It wasn't long after the death of the Prophet Muhammed and the deaths of the four Rightly Guided Caliphs that men who were greedy for power started to mistreat women once again and put them in harems.

I will no longer silently abide by rules that have been completely made up by men in order to satisfy their political, economic and sexual desires, rules that have no basis in Islam.

I put my *hijab* back on, not because a man told me to, but because it's symbolic of my identity as a Muslim woman, and of my efforts towards humbling myself before God.

I'm not a better Muslim woman because of my *hijab* and I'm no worse of a Muslim woman without it. I'll continue to wear my *hijab* with red lipstick. I'm finally free.

GLOSSARY OF ARABIC TERMS
(In alphabetIcal order)

Allah: Arabic for 'God.'

Abaya: A long-sleeved black over-garment typically made out of thin black crepe, worn by women in the Gulf on top of their clothes.

Al-Amaaken Meaning *'The Places'* which is a famous Mohammed Abdu song from the 2000s.

Alhamdulillah Meaning 'All praise is to Allah.' This is a term Muslims say to express gratitude to Allah.

Amu: Literally means a paternal uncle, but is often used by Arabs to address a man who is of a similar age of their own father as a sign of respect.

Asr : Mid-afternoon prayer, the time at which the sun starts to dip in the sky.

Assalamu alaikum: Means 'Peace be upon you,' the greeting used between Muslims.

Baba: While it's used across the Arab world as an endearing term for 'Father,' the word Baba is used in the Gulf by house servants to address their boss. It can also be used as a term to address a pimp, or the masculine half of a gay couple that's made up of a masculine gay man and an effeminate gay man.

Bint al kalb: An insult used towards females which translates to 'Daughter of a dog.'

Bisht: A black cloak, which is worn over the *thowb*, and is open at the front. It's worn by Gulf men who are members of the royal family, sheikhs, or dignitaries.

Dhuhr: Midday prayer when the sun is at its highest in the sky.

Du'aa: A personal prayer or call that a Muslim makes to Allah (God).

Dukaan: Equivalent of a small newsagents.

Eyb: This means 'Shameful.'

Egaal: A black circular headpiece made out of a hard rope-like material which is worn by Gulf men on top of their *shemaagh* or *ghutra*.

Eyni: Literally meaning 'My eye,' this is a term of endearment used in the Iraqi dialect.

Fairouz: A Famous Lebanese singer.

Fajr: Dawn prayer.

Faneela: Vest, usually worn under a *thowb*.

Gahba: Like *sharmootah* it means 'Whore' or 'Slut,' but this term is exclusively used in the Gulf Arabic dialect.

Ghishwa: A complete face veil made by taking the bottom edge of the *shayla* and draping it sideways over the face.

Ghutra: A plain white headdress worn by Gulf men.

Habibah: Means 'Girlfriend,' 'Lover' or 'Loved one' in the feminine form.

Habibty: Meaning 'My love.'

Haram: Meaning 'Forbidden.'

Inshallah: A phrase meaning 'If Allah wills.' Muslims use this phrase usually when referring to something they're going to do in the future.

Ishaa: The fifth and final prayer of the day which takes place at nightfall.

Izar: A cloth wrapped around the hips in a skirt-like fashion worn as an undergarment by both Asian and Gulf men.

Jalabiyya: A Nightdress.

Jannah: Heaven or Paradise.

Jinn: Another type of being Muslims believe in that co-exists with humans on Earth, created out of smokeless fire, invisible to the naked eye.

Jum'ah: Meaning 'Friday.' This refers to a special prayer that takes place every Friday in the mosque at midday and is obligatory for all Muslim men.

Kabsa: A popular Gulf dish consisting of rice and lamb, chicken or fish, cooked in an assortment of herbs and spices such as cloves and cardamom.

Karak: Tea made with evaporated milk, cardamom pods and a lot of sugar. *Karak* originally comes from the Indian subcontinent where it is more commonly known as chai or desi tea.

Khalas: Meaning 'Enough,' or 'That is enough.'

Khimaar: A type of headscarf that is made out of once piece of fabric, with a hole that allows it to go over the head and frame the face, and a circular hem that falls down to the waist or hip. It is worn by more conservative Muslim women.

La tahateen: This means 'don't worry.'

Ma'a salama: Literally translates to 'Go with peace' but is used interchangeably to say 'Goodbye.'

Mabrook: This means 'Congratulations.'

Maghrib: A Sunset prayer.

Majlis: A room situated on the ground floor of the house, or sometimes in an annex, where Gulf men meet and hang out, both formally and informally.

Mashallah: Literally means 'What God wills.' It is used when Muslims see something they think is commendable.

Milcha: A Gulf term for the signing of the Islamic marriage contract.

Mohammed Abdu: One of the Arab world's most famous singers from Saudi Arabia.

Niqab: The face veil.

Rashed Al-Majed: A popular Saudi Arabian singer.

Sajdah: Prostration during prayer.

Salah: Islamic prayer.

Salafi: A sect of Muslims who practice a literal interpretation of the Qur'an and sayings of the Prophet Muhammed, peace be upon him. It is a conservative and reactionary branch of Islam in which salafis aspire to practise Islam as it was practised at the time of its advent.

Sheikh: A term of respect used for the elders in Arab tribes, or for male members of Arab royal families. Sheikh can also be the term used to describe a holy man who preaches and teaches people about Islam.

Shari'ah: Islamic law as outlined in the Qur'an and the teachings of the Prophet Muhammed, peace be upon him.

Sharmootah: A slang term used in Egypt and the Levant that means 'Slut' or 'Whore.'

Shayla: A word in the Gulf dialect for a long rectangular headscarf worn by women.

Shaytan: This means 'Satan' or 'Devil.'

Shemaagh: Red and white chequered headdress worn by Gulf men.

Shukran: Meaning 'Thank you.'

Sirwaal: Thin white trousers worn under a *thowb* to hide the outline of a man's legs.

Tasbeeh: A string of rosary beads used by Muslims for remembering Allah (God).

Tayyeb: Slang word for 'Okay.'

Thowb: A white, long-sleeved shirt dress with a hem that reaches the ankles, worn by men in the Gulf.

Um: This means 'Mother.' As a sign of respect in the Arab world, a mother is addressed as 'Mother of' followed by the name of her eldest son.

Ustaadh: A term of respect used to address a teacher or a man that is considered to be knowledgeable.

Wa alaikum asalam: The reply to "*assalamu alaikum,*" meaning "and peace be upon you."

Wara' enab: Stuffed vine leaves; a popular side dish in the Arab world and the Mediterranean.

Wudu: A ritual of washing certain body parts which Muslims perform before each prayer.

Wahabbi: A form of conservative Islam followed by many people in the Arab Gulf, founded by Mohammed bin Abdul Wahhab in the 18th century, in what is modern day Saudi Arabia.

Ya: When addressing someone in Arabic, people might say "*ya Sara*" meaning "oh Sara."

Yalla: Depending on the context of the sentence, it can mean 'Go on' or 'Hurry up.'

Zift: While this literally translates as 'Asphalt,' it is used in Egypt as an insult which is equal in meaning to 'Piece of shit.'

ABOUT THE AUTHOR

Yousra Imran is half-English and half-Egyptian and grew up between London and the Arabian Peninsula. She holds a BA Hons in International Relations and is a certified personal trainer and fitness instructor. She was the fitness and wellbeing columnist for *Grazia Arabia* in 2016 and 2017 as well as a regular guest chat show host on *QBS Radio* in Qatar.

Yousra currently works and resides in West Yorkshire where she works in marketing and events in the education sector. She has been writing professionally for over ten years, with articles being published in a number of printed and online publications in the Middle East and UK. A women's rights advocate, Yousra identifies as Muslim and feminist, and is passionate about human rights and gender justice in the Middle East. Her hobbies include reading, writing and long walks in nature.

Connect with her on
Twitter: @writereadeatrepeat
Instagram: @ UNDERYOURABAYA
www.yousraimran.com